# IT'S ALL ABOUT THE
# BRAIN!

Eradicating Dyslexia, ADD, ADHD and Other Learning Challenges

By Linda Kane

The copy, photographs, and instructions in this book are for the personal use of the reader and may be reproduced for that purpose only. Any other use, especially commercial use, is forbidden under law without the written permission of the copyright holder.

Every effort has been made to ensure all information in this book is accurate; however, due to human error, differing conditions, tools, and individual skills, the publisher and the author cannot be responsible for any injuries, losses, and/or other damages which may result from the use of information in this book.

If you have any questions or comments, please contact:
    HAAF NeuroDevelopment, Inc.
    P.O. Box 13646
    Ogden, UT 84412-3646
    www.hope-future.org

Published by Mountain Star Publishing, LLC.
P.O. Box 4620, Lago Vista, TX 78645
©2020 by Mountain Star Publishing, LLC.
All Rights Reserved

Alison Quarles / Graphic Artist / Book Designer / alisonquarlesdesign.com

# Table of Contents

Dedication ................................... IV
Acknowledgments ............................. V
Foreword by Rory Feek ....................... VI
Preface ..................................... VIII
Introduction ................................ X
It's All About the Brain ..................... 1
The Blueprint ............................... 9
The Four Steps of Learning .................. 23
Eradicating Dyslexia ........................ 39
Eradicating ADD and ADHD ................... 59
Eradicating Learning Challenges ............. 85
Bipolar and Anxiety – Gone! ................. 105
It's Never Too Late for Adults .............. 119
Transformations ............................. 123
Epilogue .................................... 151
About the Author ............................ 155

## **Dedication**

Scottie, this one is for you.
If it hadn't been for you,
we would never have learned so much.

*Thank You!*

# Acknowledgments

*All glory goes to God, my Lord, Savior and Friend*
*The maker of Heaven and Earth*
*Who rejoices over us with singing!*
***Thank you for having plans and purposes for each of us.***

*The Lord your God is in your midst,*
*The Mighty One, will save;*
*He will rejoice over you with gladness,*
*He will quiet you with His love,*
*He will rejoice over you with singing.*

Zephaniah 3:17 NKJV

To Lee, my extraordinary husband, who has steadfastly stood by my side as we've journeyed this life together. Your love, friendship, prayers, and wisdom have been an anchor throughout the years. *I love you!*

To Pastor Stephen Peterson for searching out the perfect scripture for each chapter heading. The book would be incomplete without God's Word first.
**Thank you for praying for us all these years!**

To Christine Brown, Faith Haley, and Ronda Dupea who were instrumental in the tedious task of editing and proofreading this manuscript with great precision.
**Thank you for your time, talent and dedication to this book!**

To the amazing families we have had the privilege of working with at *Hope And A Future*. Your dedication, perseverance, struggles, and victories will bring much hope and encouragement to others and is a testimony of your love and faithfulness.
**Thank you for sharing your children and your stories with us!**

We are most grateful to our friend, Rory Feek, whose encouragement was a driving force behind getting this book written. One evening Lee and I were sharing our passion for getting this information shared with others and Rory just smiled. Then he quietly said, "Linda, you're an author. You just need to write the book." I repeatedly heard Rory's words of advice throughout the coming months as they had quickly become my motivation to rise early and write this book.
**Thank You! Thank You! Thank You!**

# Foreword

My wife, Joey and I first became aware of Linda and the work she does in the spring of 2014, not long after we were told that our newborn little girl, Indiana had Down syndrome. Since we had used a midwife and had the birth at home in our farmhouse, this news came as quite a surprise to us, and to most of those around us. From the beginning, the reactions from most of the people we told was, though well intentioned, that our little one was going to be more like a happy little puppy than a thriving little girl…full of unconditional love and kisses, but special. What they weren't saying, but came across just the same was, "Her abilities may be less, but her love will be more" than other children. All we knew was that we were madly in love with this perfect little gift from God.

We started working with Linda and her team when Indy was 8 months old, not long after someone passed her book, *The NeuroDevelopmental Approach* to us. Although my wife wasn't much of a reader, she read through it in an evening and handed it to me, and the next day I did the same. The approach Linda shared in those pages just made sense to us. We had already started down the same path as many DS parents, with scheduled visits to Down syndrome clinics and specialists and they all left us feeling like something must be missing. There was little, if any at all, discussion about diet, about specialized stimulation, or about other outside-the-box approaches to helping these little ones be all that they can be.

We made the three-hour drive to Jackson every four months for the next couple of years, learning new ideas and coming home with strategies we could put in place to build Indy's low muscle tone, speech, crawling and other learning delays. Before long, Indy was keeping up with other children her age in most skills, and even ahead of some kids in others. And as proud as Joey and I were of her, she was even more proud of herself. And recently, Linda has even helped one of our older daughters with some of her lifetime struggles just by changing which hand she favors and uses.

Indiana is six years old now and thriving in every way, on her way to becoming all that God meant her to be. Some of the reason for that is Linda's unique approach. I believe the foundations that Linda shares, in particular in this new book, can be game-changing for any parent whose child is struggling with Dyslexia, ADHD or other learning challenges. And any parents of kiddos with pretty little "almond eyes" like ours will see the hope and the future of their child in incredible new and life-changing ways.

**Rory Feek**
Grammy-winning singer-songwriter
New York Times bestselling author
www.thislifeilive.com

# Preface

## The Statistics Are Staggering

1 in 5 have Learning Disabilities
1 in 5 have Dyslexia
1 in 10 have ADD/ADHD
1 in 12 have Food Allergies
1 in 9 have Asthma
1 in 20 have Seizures
1 in 59 have Autism
1 in 36 (ages 3-17) have Autism
1 in 3 are Overweight

It seems that children in the 21st century are no longer learning and developing as they were meant to do, the way we did and our parents before us. Many children no longer go through the normal stages of development, the way God designed those stages to unfold. Baby and toddler innovations and gadgets, intended for good, often keep our children away from the necessary activities that all babies need, like simply spending time on their tummies on the floor and learning how to move. In this way, many parents are missing opportunities, inadvertently hindering their child in completing a strong neurological foundation from which to advance through life.

The truth is, we live in a busy world where people are moving at a pace that is exhilarating as well as exhausting. The goals we put before ourselves are challenging and daunting; we live in a time where results are demanded – fast, perfect and yesterday.

Where do our children fit into this craziness? In record numbers, our children are struggling to learn, which in turn has changed our educational system. Along the way, it was decided that the answer to these mounting learning struggles was twofold: "more" and "earlier." At the time in their lives (preschool age) when our children should be outside running and playing (which forms the foundation for their formal education), they are often being confined to a classroom packed with technology. With this, we would expect that our children would be excelling. Instead, many of them find themselves further and further behind. Instead of showing our children that learning can be an exciting adventure, teachers are being forced to focus on test results. The opportunities for expanding minds, teaching children how to think for themselves, growing in creativity, and investigating diversity, has diminished severely.

There are several fundamental rules for learning, which, unfortunately, have been usurped and ignored. The natural course of our children's development has been altered significantly in the "name of convenience" and "advancement." The solution to many learning disabilities is as simple as getting back to the most basic, foundational developmental steps. Those steps that can easily steer our children back onto a solid course, packed with much joy, fun, and hope for their future.

## Sources

*The Center for Disease Control*
www.cdc.gov

*National Center for Health Statistics*
cdc.gov/nchs/products/databriefs/db291.htm

*National Survey of Children's Health*
www.childhealthdata.org

*American Dyslexia Association*
www.american-dyslexia-association.com

*WebMD*
www.webmd.com

*MedicineNet*
www.medicinenet.com

*Dyslexia Center of Utah*
www.dyslexiacenterofutah.org

*ADDitude*
www.additudemag.com

# Introduction

Life is an exciting journey! One of the greatest joys of this journey is having children. We spend much time thinking about, dreaming about, and planning for the time when we will give our children life. We envision what will be the many "firsts" in our child's life – their first smile, their first steps, the first time we hear "Mama" or "Daddy." We picture their first day of school. We think about teaching them to drive, and about other events like their first prom and the day they leave for college. Will our daughter play sports or be a dancer? Will our son be a teacher or a preacher? We anticipate with excitement and expectation the arrival of that precious life, all while he or she grows securely in the womb.

Never in all our plans do we factor in anything less than a "perfect" bundle of joy. Our plans do not include having a child who will struggle, who we desperately want to help but cannot. Very few families escape the very real fears and hopelessness when their child is spiraling downward, either falling behind or working three times as hard as they should to keep above water. Sadly, most professionals advise that there is nothing that will change the situation for children suffering from learning disabilities and challenges – beyond teaching them coping and compensating measures.

Ignoring the situation isn't working either, because the statistics are staggering. Record numbers of children are struggling socially, behaviorally, and academically. Dyslexia, ADD, ADHD, and other learning disability labels have become commonplace and are running amok. Far too often these extremely prevalent diagnoses actually become the fixed identity of the person with the prognosis that comes with these labels. Many experts believe these disabilities are unchangeable conditions you must learn to live with; many learning disabilities are even considered diseases. The term "disease" gives the impression that there is nothing that can be done to change the situation and the life-long sentence they carry.

May I tell you dyslexia is not a disease! It is not a prognosis without hope! There is no need to live with it forever. We see dyslexia fade away all the time when the symptoms of the label are addressed actively. Likewise, the impulsivity and hyperactivity of people with ADD or ADHD does not have to be endured forever. These behaviors are nothing more than indicators. By understanding the root cause of the symptoms of these learning disabilities like dyslexia and ADD/ADHD, you can treat the cause and alter the symptoms. In fact, you can often eliminate the symptoms and, thus, remove the label entirely. Even if the symptoms are not entirely eliminated, you can improve the situation immensely. Treating some of these conditions with medication does nothing more than put a Band-Aid on the symptoms. Learning how to cope and compensate for these conditions will never bring you to the point of eradicating them. Only by addressing the root cause will you be freed from labels with all their frustrations, pain, and limitations.

Resolutions and solutions will never be found in labels, which are toxic and damaging to the future of the children who receive such labels. This happens because we live in an era where symptomatic categorization is favored rather than seeking the source of each problem. Once categorized, the symptoms are treated as if they no longer need to be changed; it merely becomes the norm for that child. The prognosis of the label then traps the child's identity, expectations are lowered, opportunities are decreased, and dreams are lost.

We see the families of labeled children every day. We hear the agonizing stories of struggle and hopelessness faced by families as they simply attempt to help their child become the person they were created to be. We hear the helplessness in their voices after they have turned everywhere, and it has not made a difference. We see the distraught look in their eyes as they tell of their child falling further and further behind. We understand and have experienced the frustration and futility of not knowing how to help our precious children. Once again, we live in a culture where labeling is the chosen practice, thinking that if something can be identified, it can be explained. Then, once we have an explanation for learning challenges, we move to routine but ineffective coping and compensating strategies. Labels abound from dysgraphia to dyscalculia, processing disorders to executive function inefficiency, dyslexia to dyspraxia, ADD to ADHD. Labels only limit! Labels are dead ends!

It does not have to be this way! There is a better way for helping children succeed despite the issues that produce these labels. The NeuroDevelopmental Approach (NDApproach – often shortened to ND) is like no other approach to human development. It is unique in its method of looking at the whole person, not at separate elements. Taking individual components, without an understanding of how they fundamentally interrelate, can severely impede a person's success in working with individuals.

As we talk with these families and explain how the NDApproach uncovers and addresses the root cause of learning issues exhibited, we see a glimmer of hope once again arise. We hear the cautious, tempered-with-excitement catch in their throats. Eager for a solution, parents want to believe! They want to let the excitement surface; they wonder whether they dare to hope again. I say to you, "*Yes, there is hope!*"

More than hope, though, **Hope And A Future** offers common sense solutions for getting to the root cause of each person's issues. Whether the child has learning disabilities that can be eliminated, or more involved, deep-rooted concerns, we give families practical advice for working with their child at home. By determining the root causes, we can develop a plan of action to lessen the effects that impact that person behaviorally, socially, and cognitively. In many cases, we can eliminate those effects entirely, along with the labels that go with them. When you determine the root cause of a learning disruption you have both hope and help. Families become empowered through the NeuroDevelopmental Approach.

Each child's potential is a direct reflection of the opportunities and stimulation presented to them. Everyone is born with a specific developmental process and blueprint that is critical to follow. Not following that developmental process is the primary cause of learning challenges, yet very few are aware of it. It is imperative to understand the brain's crucial role in development and how deviation from its "blueprint" will keep your children from reaching their full potential. There are too many adults and children, struggling through life because they don't know this fundamental design and plan. Every precious life has a God-given calling and destiny. Helping our children reach their God-given full potential so that they can successfully be about their Father's Kingdom business is why this book has come forth.

> *For I know the plans I have for you, declares the Lord.*
> *Plans to help you and not to harm you.*
> *Plans to give you a hope and a future.*
>
> Jeremiah 29:11 – New International Version

*Artist Joseph Vick*

CHAPTER ONE

# It's All About the Brain

*You formed my innermost being, shaping my delicate inside and my intricate outside...I thank You God for making me so mysteriously complex!*
Psalms 139:13-14 – The Passion Translation

The Central Nervous System (CNS) is a very complex system consisting of the brain and spinal cord. The CNS controls most of the body's function and communication. The brain is the largest and most amazing organ in the human body, made up of billions of nerve cells that communicate through trillions of connections called synapses. The organization of the brain and its incredible system of pathways is the most crucial factor in human development. A specific "blueprint" exists for how the CNS should be organized. Following that blueprint is critically imperative for a person to become neurologically organized.

Unbelievably, it is still a common belief that the brain is hard-wired, meaning that there's a point at which the brain's function ceases to improve or expand. With dyslexia, for example, it is quite common to hear from a professional that there is no way of correcting the underlying brain malfunction. This way of thinking is absolutely incorrect and outdated. The brain has an incredible amount of plasticity and redundancy. If you appropriately stimulate the brain, you will change the brain at any age. Another example where the hard-wired theory is incorrectly applied relates to ADD or ADHD. It is routinely proposed that the brain's chemistry is to blame for producing the ADD or ADHD situation. Neurodevelopmentalists vehemently disagree with this proposal, insisting that it is not the structure that determines function, but the function that determines structure. You can change the structure of the brain by inputting proper function, thus changing its chemistry. With the proper stimulation and the appropriate input, you can change both the chemistry and the intricate network of brain pathways because it is incredibly pliable. That plasticity is available as long as an individual is alive.

Modern science is catching up with what neurodevopmentalists have known since the 1940s: The brain is not hard-wired. The brain is incredibly moldable and changeable at any age.

As we read in the information above, there is incredible plasticity and redundancy in this organ. When you employ exact stimulation, you will always improve brain function. On top of that, stimulating with appropriate frequency, intensity, and duration will absolutely improve function.

The erroneous belief that structure determines the function of a person bears repeating. Inputting proper function can alter, change, and improve not only the brain's structure but that of the entire body. This knowledge means that with proper stimulation appropriately administered, you can cause disorganized and underdeveloped pathways of the brain to become organized and develop properly. It is simply a matter of knowing which areas of the brain need stimulation and exactly how to administrate it accurately.

From the moment of birth, brain cells die – every second, every minute, every day, brain cells die. Despite this, the brain increases in size. How do we account for this? The increase in the size and weight of a maturing brain is a reflection of growth in the connections between the brain cells. These connections grow through stimulation – specific stimulation. It is essential to understand that there is a massive difference between specific stimulation and random stimulation. Much of what is experienced in life is random stimulation, which will not produce change quickly or efficiently.

Random stimulation produces change almost by accident. For example, a kindergarten classroom is typically covered with loads of stimulation – colors splashed across bulletin boards and posters, items hanging from the ceiling, and walls fully decorated. Unfortunately, that particular stimulation is too scattered and random to produce learning. That "stimulation overload" causes children in that type of environment to lose a sense of who and where they are; too much random input throws the neurological system off. You can see a comparable situation in a casino with its lights, color, and noise everywhere. That kind of environment is purposely random and chaotic to disorient people and help them lose their money.

On the other hand, a room that offers little stimulation is far more successful in fostering learning. Specific stimulation, not random stimulation, is paramount to learning. With purposeful stimulation, the brain properly changes and grows. This means very precise information is introduced in a distinctly targeted way. What goes into something will determine what comes out. For example, when computers first came on the market, you could spend several thousand dollars on a model, get it home, turn it on, and still have nothing because there was no preloaded software as there is today. If you did not know how to program your computer, it was worthless; you had to input the programs and necessary information in order to use it. The brain is basically the same way. When specifically, targeted stimulation is inputted to the brain, it will improve and enhance the function in anyone.

Stimulation also needs to be given with proper frequency, intensity, and duration.

***Frequency*** means having enough opportunity and repetition so that the stimulation produces a change in the brain and becomes specific learned information. Often, we test for output without first properly inputting information.

***Intensity*** refers to the fervency of the stimulation input. It's important to be aware of this! Ask yourself, "Is the stimulation at a level to actively engage the person, or have they tuned out, having lost interest?" Without a high degree of passion, involvement, and interaction, the desired change and learning will not be achieved.

***Duration*** has a dual meaning, first referring to the length of time the stimulation is given. Contrary to traditional expectations, the shorter the duration, the higher the intensity will be. Five or ten minutes of mathematics will have a far greater impact than dragging a child through an hour of math. Intensity is lost after ten minutes at which time the stage is set for careless errors. Duration also refers to doggedness or perseverance - staying with the stimulation long enough to witness change. Specific stimulation will produce change, but it may take time, and for good reason. Frequently the stimulation is creating, developing and building new neural pathways to the brain; that effort produces internal changes that are not immediately seen. Just because immediate improvements are not evident does not mean it is time to stop offering the stimulation. Specific stimulation will produce change, and one must persevere for the required duration to see the desired outward changes.

## My Favorite Frequency, Intensity, and Duration Victory

That amazing victory involved Trey, a very sweet 12-year-old boy who had an odd way of eating his food. He would only eat food if it was *scorching hot* or *iceberg cold*. He would zap it in the microwave until the food was smoking or else, he would put it in the freezer until it was rock hard. I don't know how his teeth, tongue, or mouth handled food that way.

To address this behavior, we had his mom, Joy, do a simple activity we call "Hot and Cold Toothettes." Toothettes are little sponges on a stick that are used for oral hygiene. We asked Joy to dip the sponge into very hot water and swab it inside Trey's mouth, and then dip it into ice cold water, brushing everywhere inside of his mouth. We asked her to vary the degree of hot and cold, warm and cool over the course of time. We had her do this at a high frequency of eight to 16 times per day, for a one-minute duration each time. The temperature change added the necessary intensity. Joy was very faithful with this activity. One morning, after nearly a year persevering in this, she was quite discouraged. Trey's eating had not changed at all! Joy announced to her husband she was done; she would not and could not continue. One could not blame her for being discouraged, as moms so eagerly desire to see their children improve. Her husband convinced her, though, to keep going for a couple more weeks. After all, he reasoned, Trey's re-evaluation was coming up and Joy could discuss the disheartening situation at that time. She agreed to keep going for the two weeks until Trey's next appointment with me. She later confessed that her plan was to "...*let me have it and wring my neck.*" A few days before his evaluation, Trey woke up and ate all his food at normal temperatures. There was no buildup nor any hint of change coming. It was simply as if a switch had flipped and the light came on. All Joy could say was, "*What if I had quit a month ago? Or two weeks ago, or a day early?*" She said, "*I was ready to give up because I did not think it was working or helping.*" Then one day the connections were made complete and Trey's function became normal.

So, *Frequency* (the number of times you are inputting the information), *Intensity* (how you are inputting the information), and *Duration* (hanging in there for however long it is going to take to produce change) are all of great importance. For Trey, it took an enormous amount of input for the pathways and connections to be made. The day came when the pathways connected, the brain received the input appropriately, and normal function was established. Had Joy quit, Trey would likely still be eating his food at extreme temperatures.

You cannot have good output if the input is bad. The old adage "garbage in, garbage out" rings true here and brings us to the NDApproach. By knowing and applying our specific, appropriate input through the NDApproach, you can have significant changes in behavior and function.

# Neurological Organization Begins at Birth!

When a baby is born, he does not see or hear very well. He does not feel much, and he does not move a lot. The framework of his life is at its very beginning. The brain, with its amazing circuitry, has not developed past the very primitive reflex stage. The brain is basically a clean slate waiting to be programmed. What an exciting place for a child to be!

As that precious little one begins to move, the pathways of the central nervous system start to develop. Movement is how the brain becomes organized. Therefore, it stands to reason that movement is of vital importance to babies.

In our society today, what do we tend to do with our babies? We put them in sacks called sleepers. We swaddle them in blankets. We put them in bouncy seats and swings. We cradle them in carriers. We attach them to our bodies with a sling. We do just about everything except let them move!

Babies need to move. Every time they bang their hand or foot on a firm surface, they are sending signals to the brain, and with every signal sent, pathways to the brain are developed that will lay the groundwork of that child's future learning, interaction, and achievement.

By far, the most important place for babies during the early months of their life is lying on their stomachs. "Tummy time," as we call it, should be a major part of their everyday activities. As they are lying prone, they should be in the least restrictive of environments, which means minimal clothing and blankets – nothing that restricts movement.

Movement not only organizes the central nervous system, but it also helps to integrate the numerous primitive reflexes with which babies are born. Primitive reflexes are automatic responses that the body uses to live in utero, to come through the birthing process, and to transition into life outside the womb. These reflexes should disappear at various natural stages within the first few years of life. However, when these reflexes are not fully integrated, they end up as stumbling blocks, interfering with and preventing higher-level function from developing properly.

This information is so vital that it bears repeating. Movement is essential to the neurological development of children from the first moments of life! Then as a baby grows, there is a hierarchy of development that should be followed.

Every aspect of that hierarchy is important. For typically developing children, the changes are quite rapid within the first year of life. Watching a baby who is allowed to go through these stages of development unimpeded is fascinating. Early on, the movement of a baby will change from random and uncontrolled to volitional random movement, and with this random movement the process of organizing the central nervous system begins. Then, as the brain begins to organize itself, random movement becomes more specific.

A baby will begin by moving backward; next, they begin to pivot. Eventually they will go forward, using their arms and legs independently of one another. This movement then transitions into the most sophisticated form of movement – cross-lateral movement.

When the brain organization, that comes from lower level crawling, (what is often referred to as a "combat" crawl) has been completed, a baby should go from being on their tummy to being up on their hands and knees. At this stage you can observe the child getting used to the different feel of height and gravity. He realizes that he can look up and down. He will begin to go backward first, and then will learn to move forward. Once a baby is creeping on his hands and knees, the organization of his brain enters a higher level. All of these acts of movement and mobility have key roles in integrating primitive reflexes and in developing both hemispheres of the brain.

Every single stage of development is imperative for the future of the child. At the root of most learning issues, we find inadequacies in experiencing these developmental stages. It is important to also note that missing these stages very directly impacts visual development, which results in visual inefficiencies. On the other hand, appropriately accomplishing these stages of development puts children in the optimal place for growing, learning and developing a strong visual system.

As a side note, sitting is not a developmental step. We never encourage early sitting, as children will unfortunately achieve sitting all too soon on their own. Once sitting, children typically will do less crawling and creeping because they are happy to sit and play with the toys surrounding them. Until a child can get into and out of a sitting position on their own, their spinal cord is not strong enough to support their body weight. Thus, when we put our little ones into an unsupported sitting position, their backs will bend, putting unwanted pressure on their spines. They will usually sway back and forth a bit before crashing over. It is very important not to encourage or teach sitting before a child has properly crawled, crept, and strengthened their core muscles and spinal cord.

The next developmental step, after creeping on hands and knees, is pulling up to a standing position followed by cruising along furniture. We want to be sure that children do not go through these stages too quickly, which is the complete opposite of what many people believe is best for their child. We are in a culture that believes that the earlier a child goes from one stage to the other, the better and more "advanced" the child will be. Our current society wants to rush a child through these necessary stages of development; however, it is more important that maximum stimulation is achieved at each stage. Great patience is needed by parents to allow a baby to go through all the stages in their entirety. In our household, we have been known to gently "knock" our grandchildren down if they start to pull up on furniture too early. Once a child is cruising, it usually will not be long before they make their way to walking. Children go through many changes during that first year, and each one should happen on a timeline that's in accordance with their individualized developmental blueprint!

For children who are developing typically, it takes about 12 to 14 months to go through the stages from random movement to walking unaided. This typical development occurs naturally when children have been free to work through their developmental stages uninterrupted and unencumbered. Walkers, doorway jumpers, playpens, bouncy chairs, swings, strollers, baby carriers, and other such devices impede this proper development. Even children holding onto someone's fingers and being encouraged to walk can interrupt their proper development. You may be surprised to know that when a child walks prior to age 12 months, an underdeveloped foundation of the central nervous system often results. What this means is that a child is much more likely to have learning or attention issues, which will often surface as the child gets older.

Here is the good news! Even when a child has missed the early stages of development or effective patterning, it's not too late. It is never too late! At any time and at any age, an individual can go back and do the necessary movements that will stimulate, develop, and organize their brain. This "going back to organize" is not just for children, it also applies to adults who have experienced various types of trauma such as abuse, traumatic brain injury, stroke, etc. In these situations, the organization of the central nervous system has been disrupted and undone from injury, so recreating the activities that develop the lower levels of the brain is imperative for recovery. The stimulation to organize the lower levels of the brain must include homologous, homolateral, and cross-pattern movement.

Here's a brief look at these three types of movement:

**Homologous Movement** is when either the top half or the bottom half of the body moves at the same time, but independently from each other. For example, arms are pulling toward the body, followed by both legs pushing simultaneously.

**Homolateral Movement** is when the left side or right side moves at the same time. The left arm and left leg will maneuver, followed by the right arm and right leg. This is the movement that gets babies pivoting.

**Cross-pattern Movement** is the most sophisticated method for moving, involving both hemispheres of the brain communicating flawlessly and simultaneously. Cross-pattern movement occurs when the opposite sides of the body are being used to propel the body forward. The left arm and right leg are forward in unified movement and then in a matched motion, the right arm and left leg move to the upward position while the opposite sides are moving downward. This type of movement needs to be properly patterned, synchronized, and executed for the brain to accelerate the process of organization or reorganization of the central nervous system.

To see whether the lower levels of the brain are completely organized, you can have a child attempt to cross-pattern crawl (combat style) and cross-creep (on hands and knees). If the crawling and creeping are not properly executed, the lack of organization is evident. If the movements cannot be done correctly, the child needs to practice these daily in order to complete these stages, thus organizing the lower levels of the brain. The same thing can also be done with an adult!

Organizing higher levels of the brain without the lower levels being completely organized is like building a house without a foundation; it is simply a matter of time before it crashes. In the case of our precious children, this often means a lifetime of learning and behavioral difficulties.

CHAPTER TWO

# The Blueprint

*I will praise You, for I am fearfully and wonderfully made...*
Psalms 139:14 – New King James Version

Development is not a random act, as we discussed in the previous chapter. Rather, development is the growth of a person who has a blueprint that must be followed. If the blueprint isn't followed correctly, much like building a structure, it will contain flaws and have weaknesses. A paramount component of an individual's blueprint includes developing a dominant hemisphere, a dominant side of the brain. It is natural for everyone to have a dominant side, and this dominance is genetically coded. For the genetic coding to properly surface and be known, a person needs to go completely through the established hierarchy of development, without missing any stages. It is the hand that contains the wiring to be either right or left-side dominant. The ear, eye, and foot should follow the side their hand has chosen. If their right hand is coded as the dominant hand, then the right ear and eye should also be right-side dominant for the most efficient input of information into storage. Conversely, when the left side is the side that has been hard wired for dominance, then the left ear and eye should be the dominant ear and eye for information input and storage.

From our research and study, we have observed the genetic coding for an individual surfaces between the ages of four and seven years. The critical factor for genetic dominance surfacing is dependent upon the lower levels of the brain being organized thoroughly; this must be done through proper development, including passing through the natural stages that all babies should go through.

Babies need to be on the floor with the fewest movement restrictions possible in order to pass through these developmental stages appropriately. Why? Movement organizes the brain! *Movement proceeds cognition!* A baby's movements are all critically important!

A second key factor for the genetic coding to surface, is the stage of development when the child is using both hands. Children go back and forth between their hands in terms of dominance and that action puts gentle pressure on the brain to root out which side is the genetically coded side for dominance. Many children never go through this stage of development because they choose a dominant hand prior to the brain knowing which way fits its unique blueprint.

There are two hemispheres of the brain, popularly dubbed "left brain" and "right brain." The hemispheres should more correctly be termed "dominant" and "sub-dominant." The functions of the dominant hemisphere include logic, analytical thought, reasoning, and language (reading, writing, and speaking). The sub-dominant hemisphere directs creativity, music, and emotions. The dominant hemisphere should be the controlling hemisphere. For example, when you need emotions, the dominant hemisphere accesses them appropriately.

When someone has achieved cortical hemispheric dominance – when the side a person is "wired for," develops its natural, blueprinted dominance – the dominant hemisphere is indeed the controlling hemisphere. When cortical hemispheric dominance has not been accomplished, the brain control switches to the sub-dominant side, subverting control to the sub-dominant hemisphere, resulting in emotions "ruling" the person.

Our experience has shown, unfortunately, that many, many individuals have not established correct dominance and so haven't correctly achieved neurological organization. Without correctly established dominance in an individual, logic and reason are not ruling in their life. Chaos reigns because they are ruled by their emotions.

Choosing and using the wrong hand for dominance is a topic that is rarely, if ever, discussed outside of the neurodevelopmental field. Decades of working with individuals who have inadvertently chosen the incorrect hand for dominance has been a stunning revelation to us. The problem is significantly more widespread than we ever first realized, and it is unquestionably an important factor in children and adults not being able to break free from the struggles they are experiencing. Hand dominance is an issue of such magnitude that a good portion of this book will discuss the "handedness" issue and share case studies of the many individuals whose lives have been transformed through aligning their "handedness" with the unique blueprint for the development of their central nervous system.

As stated above, most children unfortunately favor a hand long before their genetic coding has had the opportunity to surface. This situation is a reflection of our current culture's incorrect belief that "more" education is needed, and the earlier it is done the better off the child will be. Children have lost those wonderful early years of running, jumping, and playing which facilitate their central nervous system organizing naturally. We are putting children in classroom settings at 2-3 years of age; some have crayons in their hands even earlier than that! We have not given our children the opportunities they need for the lower levels of their brains to organize so that their genetic coding can surface. In my generation, children were outside playing at all possible waking hours. We were creative, imaginative, and always on the go; our parents almost had to drag us inside when darkness fell. Today's youngsters spend countless hours with the electronic screens of computers, tablets, gaming systems, educational toys, and phones. The opportunity for fresh air, sunshine, movement, and creativity has decreased tremendously for them.

Many factors reveal a person's genetically coded dominance. As neurodevelopmentalists, we look at the lower-level organization, the functional output of the individual, the emotionality of the individual, as well as his or her academic function. We do not recommend switching dominance lightly nor quickly. The decision to do so is a result of putting together many pieces of a particular puzzle. We highly recommend considering a change in dominance only when working with a neurodevelopmentalist who is highly trained in examining and analyzing all the pieces of this complex puzzle.

Again, everyone is genetically coded to be either left or right-side dominant. Not using the hand of a person's genetic blueprint will undoubtedly negatively affect the rest of their life. Switching sides to align their dominance properly is absolutely worth the effort! We have changed the handedness of many adults, resulting in establishing correct dominance alignment. Unlike younger children, adults are well able to articulate the differences they note in their lives. For example, some adults have reported coming off medications they had been taking to help them cope with life. All have mentioned how much clearer they were able to think. These adults also relayed significant stress reduction and were thrilled with how ordered their lives had become. I worked with one 21-year-old who could not pass her driver's license test; she had flunked the test four times! After her dominance was switched entirely, (hand, ear, eye, and foot) and had become aligned on the left side, she passed her test with a near-perfect score.

One desperate gentleman came to us feeling like his life was falling apart. He explained that he felt like a juggler who was attempting to keep all the plates spinning on the ends of poles. He could no longer keep everything going in his life and thought he was headed for a nervous breakdown. He was a highly successful businessman, husband, and father; however, as he had grown older, his life had become harder. Hormones change as we age. Job responsibilities typically become more complex. His family size increased every couple of years for a number of years. Many factors were continuing to add to this man's stress level, and because of his incorrectly aligned dominance, he was unable to cope with them well. When someone goes against their unique genetic coding, things do not just randomly improve with time or even with experience; instead, all the compensatory patterns that have been developed become even more difficult. When this man switched his hand and completed his natural dominance, the change was amazing. His wife kept saying that he was an entirely different person. His stress level dramatically reduced; he was able to multi-task for the first time in his life, and his natural state had changed to one of being calm in all situations!

One woman who changed her handedness and appropriately lined up her dominance to her genetic coding was amazed at how orderly her household had become. Her husband had taken "before and after" pictures of their home, unbeknownst to her. In the "before" pictures, the kitchen and bathroom counters were utterly cluttered. In the pictures her desk was laden with piles of paper and books. She could not even enter her bedroom's walk-in closet and could barely open the hall closet without the risk of being bombarded with falling objects. However, the "after" pictures showed a completely different household. The new photos were of a home with everything neatly and effortlessly organized. Establishing her correct dominance radically changed this woman's entire lifestyle.

Another woman who changed her handedness and correctly lined up her dominant side, was amazed at her increased energy since the change. She was also surprised by how much work it had taken to compensate for the inefficiencies of her neurological disorganization. In her forties, she felt like she had more energy than ever before.

Occasionally, it appears that the problems experienced could be solved with a hand-switch, when in actuality, that is not the solution. However, in these situations, the process of switching to the wrong hand eventually causes the dominance to shake out and provokes the body to organize itself correctly.

One young man who worked very hard to get his dominance lined to the right, found that his dominance just would not align. After a year, the neurodevelopmentalist working with him switched this young man to his left side in an effort to achieve dominance, thinking that if his body would not organize to the right side then he must be genetically coded to be left-side dominant. His history also had revealed that he had not chosen a dominant hand by second grade so his teacher unfortunately determined he should do everything right-handed. Ready to be past the learning struggles, this family began transitioning their son to left-side dominance. Shortly after that, his family moved into my area and I began working with them. After two evaluations, I believed that left-side dominance was incorrect for this boy because his body gave multiple signals to indicate otherwise. I felt terrible telling them they needed to switch him back to the right. As difficult as it was, it was necessary and turned out to be correct! Four months later, this young man was completely right-side dominant. What would not come in on previous attempts actually slid in very quickly the second time around. The parents are convinced it would not have happened without the attempt to go left, because something "clicked" when they pressed his system the wrong way, which then allowed his dominance to establish. Though they had worked on right-side dominance for more than a year, it did not come in until their endeavor to go the *other direction* failed, and then they returned to attempt it again. While it is not always understandable, we have seen this happen multiple times. It appears that going the *wrong way* may sometimes be a positive step. When an individual is trying to achieve dominance on an incorrect side of the body, be assured the body will absolutely let us know.

Here's an analogy I use when I recommend that someone switch dominance: I have flown between Salt Lake City and Boston three times per year for more than 10 years. The flight from Boston to Salt Lake City sometimes takes 4.25 hours, sometimes it takes 5 hours, and sometimes it takes 5.5 hours. Each time, it is the same flight pattern, same airline, and the same time of day. Someone going against his or her genetic coding is like the flight that takes the longest amount of time – which is when the plane is flying into strong headwinds. In this case, the plane is vigorously buffeted and the engines have to work very hard; everything is slowed down because it takes much more effort. By contrast, the flight that requires the middle amount of time is like having properly aligned genetic coding but not having ear, eye, and/or foot dominance wholly lined up. Progress will take longer but won't be as difficult as the longest flight. Of course, being completely dominant with everything aligned on the correct side is like the quickest flight – the plane has tailwinds that help it along; it is not being buffeted; the engine works with ease; the flight is much quicker and easier, and everything flows smoother and better. Achieving genetically correct dominance in an individual streamline the mind and body to function together with more efficiency, with less effort and the ability to do everything much more quickly.

We have a lot of experience helping children and adults become their "true selves." It has been remarkable and our privilege to witness the changes and transformations in the lives of many children. The children have not "hated" their parents for encouraging them to change their dominance, though it was hard work and there was a lot of "building muscle memory" involved. Muscle memory is something developed through training: the hand that brings the fork or spoon up to the mouth is a muscle memory activity. The hand that is used for throwing a ball, washing the windows, and brushing teeth are all examples of activities that develop muscle memory. Practicing handwriting produces muscle memory in the fingers and hand. If an individual will set their mind to switching a hand, the change can actually be quite fast.

When considering a hand change, the important thing is to keep a positive attitude about it. You can talk about switching hand dominance with your child like it is the most exciting adventure there is! After all, becoming who God created them to be IS exciting. The genetic coding has been pre-determined in their DNA, which makes it God's choice whether one is left or right-handed. The decision for which hand one uses is neither the parent's nor the child's to make. It is God's and we *know* God does not make mistakes.

There will be a period of adjustment when changing handedness and dominance. There can also be a period of *more* confusion and disorganization as the brain switches everything from one hemisphere into the other hemisphere. It is quite an enormous undertaking. I had one 14-year-old who came to me with a bipolar label. After some time, this young man "lost" the label but continued to have some "quirks." During the process of working together, he was supposed to, but would NOT change his hand. I finally told his mom there was no reason for him to continue coming for re-evaluations if he would not change his hand dominance, as there was nothing more we could do for him. It really bothered her that her son still had issues, although nothing like he previously had, and she knew that she needed to find a way to convince him to change his hand dominance. She decided to offer him $300 if he would make the hand change and that was all it took. He switched hands, aligned his dominance and all of his oddities faded away.

Although most periods of adjustment are relatively brief, with 2-4 weeks being the average, the change in hand usage brought a significant upheaval for this young man. His adaptation included slipping back into bipolar type behaviors, even as far as putting holes in the walls again. He was way off his "new normal" and was doing things the family had not seen in two years. This behavior continued for two and a half months. At one point I told his mom she did not have to proceed with the hand change, but she was determined. She said that for the first time, her son was able to remember math facts. She used this as her encouragement that they were truly on the correct path with the hand change. His alarming behavior continued for another two weeks, and then reorganization happened. He became entirely who God had created him to be – a wonderful, polite, self-controlled young man. He was transformed into an amazingly tender and loving uncle to his young niece, with whom he could now be left alone. We saw a young man emerge who smiled a lot and was relaxed, joked often, and was happy. Sadly, his mom, who was his most prominent advocate and encourager, died just a couple of years later. I often wonder who would be there now for him if he was still the violent, depressed young man trapped in the bipolar label that he had been.

We also worked with two sisters who were both incorrectly using their right hands for dominance. As a result, both of them were having academic, social, and processing concerns. The primary goal for the older sister was to "unlock language." The main desire for the younger sister was to be able to attend and focus better, as well as to be less distracted and forgetful. Upon graduation from the NDApproach program, the mom commented that her older daughter was much more comfortable and at ease when conversing. The girl's ability to express her thoughts and feelings had also greatly improved, and she had matured immensely. She was much more confident, outgoing, and delightful. About her younger daughter, the mom commented that this daughter's hyperactivity, distractibility, and impulsivity had been significantly reduced. Mom also noticed that the younger girl's attention and focus had increased exponentially.

It was very interesting to have changed the hand dominance of several artists, where significant levels of skill had been developed. One had recently graduated from a renowned art institute. Art was her passion and occupation; she had spent many, many years developing her talent. After developing new muscle memory and bringing up her skill levels with her left hand, she became a better artist than when she was incorrectly using her right hand. Significant improvement in the artwork was notable with each artist!

We have seen the same kinds of results when people, who were very sports-involved, changed their hand dominance. Whatever the sport being played, when correct dominance was established and skill levels developed on the dominant side, the performance of the player was far superior to the level at which they played prior to the switch.

That was the case with Tim, a young man who struggled with fetal alcohol syndrome. Tim was the worst ballplayer on his high school baseball team. In fact, the coach allowed Tim on the squad because he was such a great guy and so desired to play. After Tim switched his hand and completed dominance organization, the coach marveled, *"Never in thirty years of coaching have I ever seen such dramatic improvement! Tim has gone from the worst player on my team to the best player! He is our star pitcher."* Conversely, we had another boy who already was the best player on his baseball team. When his hand changed and dominance changes were completed, his skill level advanced even higher.

When we improve a person's central nervous system organization and function, there may be long-established habits that need to change, too. Keep in mind, though, that once the brain is neurologically organized, establishing good, healthy habits is much easier. It takes time, practice, and patience to develop a dominant hand different from what was being used, but those who have done it, have never regretted it.

Is changing hand dominance worth it? Yes, absolutely! While the person undergoing the change may not be happy about the work at the outset, they are always grateful that they rose to the challenge and made the switch when they reflect on the differences they can see in themselves. Accomplishing the correct, genetically coded dominance offers lifelong positive effects that can be achieved through no other means.

This exactly was the case with Cara. She was 16 when I first met her and was an emotional wreck. She cried for hours, sometimes all day long. Cara was homeschooled, thankfully, for she would have never been able to handle a traditional school setting. When something upset her, she would go cry for a couple of hours. Cara told me that she had to work very hard to pull herself together just to attempt more schoolwork; nearly everything in her life was hard. Even knowing that it would help her immensely, she was very resistant to changing dominance. She regularly fought wearing an eye patch or occlusion glasses (glasses worn to encourage the correct eye to become dominant).

Cara told me the day came when her mom absolutely refused to battle anymore about the eye occluding and literally tackled her to the ground and put a Band-Aid eye patch on her. Cara reported how much more comfortable using the Band-Aid was and how grateful she was that her mother loved her enough to see her through this. Once Cara *decided* to become left-side dominant, it happened quite rapidly. Cara became fully left-side dominant, and in the process, her life changed forever for the better.

A couple of months after Cara had completely established her left-side dominance, this e-mail came to me from her mom, Diane.

> *Dear Linda,*
> *This is a "happy" for you.*
>
> *I want to tell you that my dear and precious Cara (who I knew was always in that body somewhere) has emerged!!*
>
> *What a delight and a joy she has become. No longer are we plagued with continual crying and meltdowns, yelling and screaming, disrespect and dishonor. Our home continues to evolve into a place of peace and joy and laughter. No more walking on eggshells waiting for explosions. Aaahhh the bliss and joy.*
>
> *Cara can actually see the difference in herself. We talk about what life was like and how life is now. She is so much more grounded and in control of herself. She is doing very well in track and surprising herself by her success. She is so happy. Life is not perfect, but it is normal. All praise to God our healer!*
>
> *Hope this finds you encouraged. Keep on...*

Two months later, I saw Cara for what I hoped would be her graduation evaluation. We always want to make sure the dominance change is complete, without any regressions before they graduate. When Cara walked in, I nearly fell over. Before me stood a very mature, capable and confident young woman. All the immaturity of four months ago was completely gone. Diane told me that Cara was going to their church camp (over a thousand miles away) as a camp counselor for the summer, remarking that there was no possible way Cara could have done this, four months earlier. That summer apparently was highly successful and great fun. Cara also decided she wanted to attend college. Her future was ready and wide open for whatever she chose to do. She was fully capable now of facing whatever she encountered, or so we thought...

I received this email from Cara four years after she successfully completed her neurological organization, or more aptly, reorganization, and had become fully left-side dominant.

> Hi Linda,
>
> I hope you're well. I know it's been a long time since you've seen me, but I am wondering if you'd be able to help me. I know I graduated Program totally left-handed. However, I have switched myself back to being right-handed because I couldn't be creative when I was using my left hand. I literally couldn't have creative thoughts.
>
> I am going to College for Creative Studies in Detroit. I moved here last May and have been doing well in school and know that graphic design is what I'm supposed to be doing. However, my emotions are all over the place and I also feel like it takes me a long time to accomplish projects. I have a hard time managing my stress levels.
>
> My question is this: would it be worth it to occlude and try and get myself back to being left? What do I do about the creativity? I'm literally being paid at times for my handwriting when I do chalkboards and painting (my freelance sign work). I know that when I was left, so many things emotionally were better for me. I want to get back to where I'm in control of my body and emotions versus them being in control of me.
>
> Do you have any advice for me?
>
> Thank you so much!
>
> Cara

Cara knew the answer to her question without ever asking it. I strongly encouraged Cara to return to left-handedness, as you can see in my reply to her.

*Cara,*

*Yes, yes, yes....... switch yourself back to being all left-side dominant. Your creativity will come. It will. You will be even more creative. It just needs to go through the developmental steps for that left-hand. Plus, this may be a seed that falls to the ground and dies so that God can resurrect the masterpiece He has planned for you.*

*Please keep in touch and let me know how you are doing. Being left-side-dominant is going with your body's blueprint and truly the only good choice.*

*Blessings and love ... Linda*

I never heard back from Cara. I attempted to contact her but never was successful. After many months I contacted Cara's mom. Diane reported sorrowfully that Cara was unwilling to do the work to become left-side dominant and had sadly left college. She was working at a health food store with no plans to return to school. Cara had been doing very well in her first traditional school setting, after homeschooling through high school. She was making all A and B grades until she switched back to using her right hand. Then, her grades began dropping, and her emotions once again had taken over.

The comments from Cara's evaluation in April 2013, when she tested entirely left-side dominant were incredible, and a testimony to all the hard work this family had done.

The evaluation notes read:
- Motivated to catch up on schoolwork, finish high school
- No bad days!
- Emotions, behavior significantly matured, typical of 18
- Has not had a meltdown in a very long time
- Rolls with life much better
- Discerns friendships and what is appropriate
- Tactility responses within the normal range
- Not as jumpy
- No longer says she doesn't like people touching her
- Hearing people better

- Visualization skills improved
- Left handwriting appearance and speed improved
- Vital capacity improved
- Vestibular system normalized
- Endurance and coordination normalized

My prayer is that Cara will one day remember all the benefits and improvements she had after she aligned with her body's blueprint and will return to being left-handed. It is never too late!

Not all children resist and fight hand dominance change. I recently evaluated three children who completely switched their hand dominance in four months.

Nathan, a precious 21-one-year-old young man we worked with, is another example of someone who eagerly embraced hand-changing. We met Nathan at a conference where he was a speaker. He was quite accomplished and very passionate about life, and he enthusiastically did public speaking about an organization he supported that worked worldwide on humanitarian issues. Nathan also has Down syndrome.

At Nathan's initial evaluation, we found he was supposed to be left-side dominant. Early on in school, Nathan had been going back and forth with manual function, using both hands to write. The determination was made to teach him to write with his right hand. Quite often we have seen this to be the default. When children are using both hands after the age of eight, it merely means the genetic coding has not yet surfaced as it should have. Not enough crawling and creeping has been done to fully organize the lower levels of the brain. That was the situation with Nathan.

When I told Nathan and his mother that he needed to become left-side dominant, Nathan was excitedly agreeable. He was determined to use his left hand for everything if it was going to help him. Nathan embraced switching to his left with zealous determination.

Nathan had the bad habit of biting his fingernails and picking at both his finger and toenails. Two weeks after switching his dominance to the left side, this habit completely disappeared. He loved bowling but had been unable to bowl right-handed without using the left hand to support the bowling ball. He often curved the ball into the gutter. His first time bowling left-handed was quite remarkable. He could hold the bowling ball with his left hand alone and got the best score he had ever achieved. Nathan also noted that he was so much calmer. At times, prior to switching, he would become over-excited, elevating his voice too loudly and feeling a bit out of control. After switching to using his left hand, his ability to handle his excitement had totally normalized.

The substantial, severe impact of using the incorrect hand for dominance cannot be overstated. The majority of this chapter came from Chapter Nine of my first book, The NeuroDevelopmental Approach. There is Hope…And A Future! In the five years since that book was published, I have seen a dramatic increase in the number of people who are negatively impacted by having incorrect hand dominance. I believe this relatively unknown catastrophe regarding handedness is of epic proportion - and it's the cause of many people not living the lives they are meant to live. The stories and case studies we will share throughout this book (all names have been changed for the privacy of each family) detail the significant impact that aligning with one's blueprint truly makes.

CHAPTER THREE

# The Four Steps of Learning

*God is trying to teach us, letter by letter, line by line, lesson by lesson.*
Isaiah 28:10 – Good News Translation

Before going any deeper into our discussion of the life-altering effects of neurological organization and the genetic coding for dominance, it is necessary to understand how every person learns. Any deviation from this pattern will contribute to the overall negative symptoms those with learning issues experience.

A recent movement in learning focuses entirely on learning styles, with the objective of ascertaining whether a child learns better through visual, auditory, or tactile channels. There is new writing out about more learning styles, but these are the ones I would like to focus on. Once the learning style or preference has been determined, teaching is directed toward that learning style. This approach is as challenging for the teacher with a classroom of 30 children, who inevitably differ drastically in learning styles, as it is for the homeschooling family with children of differing learning styles. It is true that some children learn better visually while others learn more efficiently through auditory information, and still some children are quicker to learn kinesthetically. However, such preferences are due to a neurological imbalance. Understanding this, we can appreciate that it is far better to organize the central nervous system, which will allow children to excel in all modes for learning. Math processes are a visual function and are best taught visually. Math facts are an auditory process – they are thought as they are used – and are best taught audibly. Science learning is made more concrete through the use of kinesthetic projects. So, you can see that striving to ascertain how a child learns best is well-intentioned, but children are best served by becoming superior learners in every modality of study, using all five physical senses.

Learning consists of four steps: **First**, the brain receives information. **Next**, the brain processes the information it has received. **Third**, after processing, the brain stores the information. **Finally**, in order for information to be of any benefit, the brain has to use it. This four-step pattern for learning is the same for every healthy and typically developing person, as well as for persons with a brain injury, genetic interferences, or other complications: receive, process, store, and use. We will look at each one more closely.

***The 1st step*** for learning is to get information into the brain that was not previously there. A person receives information through their senses of touch, taste, smell, temperature, seeing, and hearing. Input then produces output. If the brain does not receive the information accurately, it will never output that information correctly. When the central nervous system is disorganized, it will not receive information correctly and thus, input and subsequently the output will be confused. As a result of this disorganization, you will have a very frustrated child who is unable to function as he should.

Touch or tactility is critically essential for every human being. At birth, babies communicate almost entirely through their skin. Babies who receive skin-to-skin contact are more relaxed; they cry less, sleep well, and breastfeed more easily. Touch increases the immune system, lowers cortisol levels, and stimulates a sequence of proper hormonal changes. It is a fact that babies who are deprived of skin-to-skin contact fail to thrive, lose weight, and eventually die a premature death.

Many tactile receptors send information to the brain. For example, there are deep pressure and light surface awareness as well as tactile receptors for temperature awareness, taste, and the sense of smell. These signals can sometimes be distorted, and the distortion can be either **hyposensitive** or **hypersensitive**. Often, the result of hyposensitivity is: if you cannot feel it, you cannot use it.

Hyposensitivity to surface touch can be quite dangerous. Children need to feel pain to alert their parents that something is wrong. Children need to know when they have cut themselves, have a raging ear infection, broken a bone, or have an insect biting them.

When the deep sense of touch is *hypo*sensitive, (they can't feel deep level pain well) you have children who interact too roughly. These are the children you brace yourself for as they are running toward you to hug you because they may knock you over! Children who wet the bed are almost always hyposensitive at the deep-pressure level. They simply do not feel the sensations urging them to use the restroom and usually have an immature central nervous system, which puts them into a "too deep" sleep pattern. A lesser degree of hyposensitivity to touch can be observed with someone who holds a pencil in a heavy-fisted grasp. A parent can spend seemingly endless discussion with their child about the importance of holding a pencil correctly, all while giving them ample demonstration, to no avail. It takes the intensity of this "death grip" for their brain to receive the information and have the ability to hold the pencil. When the tactile information is not received correctly, the appropriate output is impossible despite how much you talk with and teach a child about proper responses and behavior.

On the other hand, for *hyper*sensitive children, (they feel pain too much) life can be quite challenging. For them, the tags in shirts need to be cut out, and sock seams must be perfectly straight on the toes, when you can get them to wear socks! With nail trimming, their reaction is so dramatic one would think that their fingertips were being clipped off. Often, children who have hypersensitive surface tactility will only wear "soft" or "comfy" clothing; jeans and dress slacks can be absolutely unacceptable to them.

Another common dilemma with the tactile system concerns the trigeminal nerve. It is one of the largest nerves in the body, sending all information from the eyes, ears, nose, mouth, and face to the brain. It stands to reason that this nerve is critical for a child's function and learning. Inefficient input of information at this level can disrupt language development, visual development, auditory development, and can also be a factor in picky eating, amongst other things.

***The 2nd step*** for learning is processing information. As soon as the information is received, the brain should begin to process and analyze that information. Processing information is the equivalent of short-term memory; the brain has to process the data with short-term memory before it can shift into long-term memory. Information processed incorrectly is very detrimental; we see a myriad of problems caused by inefficient auditory and visual processing. Once these inefficiencies exist, the effects are immediately noted and only compound with age.

Learning to process sequential auditory information well is imperative. Sequential processing is the number of pieces of information a person can get into short-term memory, retain, and then relay back in the exact order given. It is the basis for social skills, the foundation for behavior, and reveals a person's developmental age. When a child has poor auditory processing skills, there are a multitude of negative ramifications.

A one-year-old should be able to process one piece of information. For example, you should be able to tell a one-year-old to "clap hands" and have her respond by clapping her hands. Or, you can ask her to touch her nose, and she touches her nose. In church nurseries, you can quickly identify the one-year-olds who are not often away from their mothers. They are the hardest to watch because all they do is cry. No matter what you do, they cry and cry because all they can think of is Mom; they are processing one piece of information involving the world around them.

A two-year-old should be able to process two pieces of information, such as touch hair and ear, or clap hands and wave bye. Two-year-old processing is "I want" and "don't want" and is where the "terrible twos" tantrum originates. At one year old, a child who is processing one piece of information could be in a nursery playing nicely with a toy. Even if another child came and took that toy, the first child would be okay; he would just go on to the next toy. At two years old, however, the same child would fight unreasonably if his toy were taken. It would require much consoling or redirecting for him to move on from his stuck position.

Once children are three years old, they should be able to process three pieces of information. They are past the terrible twos; they can maneuver past the "I want" to realize there is another option or a consequence to their behavior. A three-year-old should be able to repeat words to assess their processing skills. You can ask them to say "ball, car, truck" or "orange, green, pink" and they will do so. Three-year-olds especially like Simon Says-type games: "Simon says, jump, turn around, salute."

A four-year-old should be able to process four pieces of information. A five-year-old should process five pieces of information, and a six-year-old should handle six pieces. Seven pieces of sequential information is where most people achieve average processing ability. Phone numbers were originally seven digits long to match the average processing ability. When working with the higher sequences, we usually use numbers. You say the numbers in a monotone voice, to a one-second beat. Testing the sequential ability to process information is part of some IQ testing. Digit-span testing is commonly used to assess a person's ability, but unbelievably, it isn't used to further it.

An individual's level of processing directly impacts how well they function in every circumstance of their life because it affects how they see and interpret the world around them. Children do not need to be limited to the status quo. Getting their processing as high as you can, as soon as you can, is an invaluable gift you can give them.

Auditory processing is of key importance for reading. An individual must be able to process five pieces of sequential information strongly, and six pieces of information weakly, in order to have the ability to learn to read phonetically. A child unable to process at this level is painful to listen to as they attempt to sound out words. Reading "cat" can come out C----Aaaa----T. C---Aaaa---T. C-Aa--Kangaroo. We have seen many families who have purchased every phonics program on the market without getting good results. That's because it is not the method that makes the difference; what matters is getting a child's processing high enough so the brain can put the pieces together.

Low processing sets a child up for failure, both academically and socially. She is unable to keep up with conversational language and directions from parents or teachers. Typically, an average sentence is seven to eight words in length. An individual not able to process that many pieces of information is at a severe disadvantage. What words out of each sentence does she hear and process? Which words are left out? You can see that there is a massive difference between "Jessie, do not run in the store," and "Jessie, run in the store."

Now, think of the typical kindergarten class, with lots of activity and movement. These classrooms usually have many different, high-intensity stations that the students rotate through, spending a very short time at each. That is how you maintain the interest, attention, and focus of a five-year-old. When you talk to them, you get down to their level. You deliberately make eye contact and gain their undivided attention. You give them very short, easy-to-process sentences followed by, "Do you hear me?" Consider what happens when a 12-year-old who is processing at this level is in a classroom where the teacher says, "Students, I want you to take out your math book, turn to page 32 and do problems 10 through 20 at the bottom of the page." That young man might hear, "Take out math book – turn." Or he might hear "Math book – page 32 – problems." He might be looking at his neighbor to see what to do, which page to turn to or asking, "What are we supposed to do?" He will only get bits and pieces of the directions given to him and he will be lost about what he is being asked to do. Individuals in this position are unable to process conversational language thoroughly and efficiently.

By the time you can sequence seven pieces of information into and back out of short-term memory, you should be able to process conversational language without problem. There are many children who are not processing conversational language, and there are also a lot of adults who are not processing conversational language. Years ago, people talked to each other a lot. They sat around the dinner table and not only spoke to each other, but they listened with interest. Families listened to programs and stories on the radio. They did not live today's fast-paced lifestyle. There were no video games, televisions and endless sports to participate in or watch. A scene I have witnessed numerous times in airport restaurants is a common portrait of our culture today: The family sits at a table, with Dad reading the newspaper, Mom reading a book, and each child playing with a tablet or video game; not once do they engage with each other. The opportunities for developing good, let alone excellent auditory processing skills are not in practice today as they were in the past.

Sadly, there are many in this generation, especially many children, who are unable to sit in a classroom and attend because developmentally, they are still at a four- or five-year-old level. They are still processing the way a kindergartner would, but without the direct eye contact and short sentences being offered. How would you get a four- or five-year-old to sit through a second grade or higher classroom? Not just sit there, but sit there for seven hours a day and participate? I suggest you would have to drug them; and that is precisely what we are doing. Our culture is dispensing medications at an alarming rate in order to get children to attend and sit still in a classroom where they are not developmentally ready to be. Unfortunately, this has become standard procedure. Medications to control symptoms have become long-term solutions, which were never meant to be.

Medication attacks the central nervous system; it is not a positive thing. Amphetamines and methylphenidates are stimulants commonly used for treating ADD/ADHD attention issues. Stimulants only relieve symptoms temporarily and definitely are not a cure.

Many children (and adults) are taking Ritalin, Adderall, Concerta, Dexedrine, Vyvanse, or other stimulants to control impulsivity and aid attention and focus issues. These drugs are dangerous and have a myriad of side effects, the most common of which include insomnia, nervousness, nausea, drowsiness, loss of appetite, weight loss, headaches, restlessness, vomiting, irritability, anxiety, and dizziness. More severe side effects include hallucinations, confusion, tremors, seizures, racing heartbeat, shortness of breath, chest pain, blurred vision, buzzing in ears, and motor tics.

All of these drugs warn of serious, possibly fatal, heart and blood pressure problems. All warn they are habit-forming. They admit long-term usage could lead to drug dependency and possible withdrawal symptoms when stopped.

Strattera is a medication for the treatment of focus, attention and impulsivity issues; it is not a stimulant. Even so, it too has many side effects, including headaches, sleepiness, and agitation. More serious side effects include a worsening of the original symptoms it is supposed to be helping, not to mention suicidal thoughts and attempts, anxiety, panic attacks, sleep trouble, restlessness, hallucinations and delusions.

I offer this not as a condemnation for those who have turned to the use of medication in an attempt to help their child, but as a concern for this being the first and foremost treatment plan offered to parents. It is treating symptoms. It is not getting to the root cause of the problem because these medications do not - and cannot – train the brain to process information. The NDApproach gets to the root cause of the problem. There are no dangerous side effects to implementing an NDApproach program. It is a non-invasive, systematic way to eliminate the symptoms that are wreaking havoc in the individual's life.

A very common scenario we see involves bright 11, 12, or 13- year-olds who come to us with attention and learning concerns. These smart young people are not able to sit and handle the classrooms they are in for hours every day. Unable to process more than four or five pieces of information, they have lost confidence in their true abilities. In addition, there are almost always sensory issues that interfere. For example, the socks in their shoes are not lined up, or the tags in their shirts are driving them crazy. It may be that the marker smell holds their attention, or they hear the plane overhead or the birds chirping outside the classroom window. They may use too much of their peripheral vision so that a boy flipping a pencil nearby is as much a distraction as the girl who is twirling her hair. No wonder they cannot concentrate and focus! The indictment needs to be against the established protocol of drugging our precious children instead of fixing the fixable dysfunctional central nervous system.

**Visual processing** refers to how many pieces of visual information a person can put into short-term memory, retain, and correctly give back in proper order. As with auditory processing, visual processing correlates to the developmental age and abilities of a person. A one-year-old should be able to process one piece of visual information. A child should increase one sequential piece of information per year until the age of seven. Then, at seven years old, processing seven pieces of sequential information, a child arrives at average visual processing.

Symptomatically, visual processing problems with younger children can be noticed when there is an inability or inconsistency in recognizing or learning letters, numbers, and words. Older children with visual processing problems may have trouble with math, spelling, reading, visual attention, and picking up visual information. With math, for example, it is quite challenging to accomplish long division without the ability to sequence the steps correctly. Spelling, in large part, is holding the picture of a series of letters. Those who visually process at a younger age level will have the attention span of their developmental ability and age, just as with auditory processing.

Working on your child's processing ability will significantly impact their maturity, behavior, and academic ability. Reaching a span of seven is average; however, facilitating your child to achieve past average into superior function should be the goal. When an individual can sequence, or hold together, 10 pieces of information, she has the ability to learn instantaneously. Everything she is hearing and seeing processes into short-term memory immediately. As long as her long-term memory is functioning well, she will need to do minimal studying.

**The 3rd step** for learning is the storage of information. Learned information is primarily stored through visual and auditory channels.

An individual is born with two ears, but only one of those should be used as the primary pathway for the input of information to the brain for storage. The other ear is used peripherally, always monitoring the background noise. As an example of this dual path in action, imagine that you are listening to a speaker and several babies are crying in a nearby nursery. You are not paying any attention – at least not until your baby starts crying. When that happens, you instantly snap to attention. That's because the subdominant ear picked up your baby's crying while your dominant ear was listening to the speaker.

There is a similar division of labor for our two eyes. The dominant eye's pathway is designed for the input of information for storage in the dominant side of the brain. While we continually use both eyes for depth perception, teaming, tracking, and convergence, only one eye should be used for storing information into long-term memory.

All learned information is designed to be inputted into the same-side eye and ear. The data then crosses over and will be stored in the dominant hemisphere of the brain where logical thinking, analytical thinking, reasoning, and language occurs. When that information is needed, the pathways are appropriately connected to that hemisphere of the brain, and retrieval of the information will be quick and effortless. A person who is not aligned entirely on one side or the other is said to be mixed-dominant, resulting in information being stored haphazardly and not always being immediately accessible.

For example, if a child keeps all his books and toys neatly on shelves, finding a specific book will be quick and easy. If he stores all his toys and books in a toy chest, he may have a harder time finding a book. He may empty half his toy chest before seeing it or, he may find it closer to the top. On some days he may empty everything out of the chest and still not find the book, even though he knows it was definitely there. It is the same with information learned. Some days you know what you have learned; other days you do not. Inconsistent information recall is one of the most frequent symptoms of mixed dominance.

Neurological organization is not complete when just the eye, ear, and hand dominance are aligned. There also needs to be a dominant foot. The dominant foot is the foot you kick with, hop on, and lead with when walking, running, etc. Which foot goes into pants first or goes up the stairs first? Which foot is the power foot for skating, scootering, and snowboarding?

Unfortunately, many things in our society and environment interfere with becoming neurologically organized. Many children and adults never achieve dominance. Their systems attempt to adjust through compensatory methods of dealing with the inefficiencies, and some individuals will compensate better than others. The severity of the mixed dominance, as well as the processing ability, factor strongly in how much the neurological disorganization will impact a person's function. Function affects every aspect of life.

Numerous problems arise from having mixed dominance, because when a person is disorganized on the inside it is nearly impossible to be organized on the outside. A mixed-dominant person will usually display inefficiency in two different extremes – either being totally disorganized or hyper-organized. If disorganized, there may be piles and stacks throughout the home or office; the bedroom and closets are likely disaster areas. The person knows something is there, but just cannot seem to find it. Disorganized, mixed-dominant people lose glasses, car keys, and just about anything they set down. On the other hand, a hyper-organized, mixed-dominant person compensates for disorganization by keeping possessions excessively organized, with a place for everything, and it better be in that place when they go to retrieve it.

The most prevalent symptom of mixed dominance is inconsistent recall of information. Quite simply, information that is not stored correctly will not readily be accessed. Visual information stored in the subdominant hemisphere creates the most common symptom of dyslexia – information reversals. The information is stored in the wrong hemisphere, and when the person goes to retrieve it, it cannot be found. Instead, the brain has to go searching. Then, once the information has been located, the brain must take that information and put it into the proper hemisphere for use. This complicates the process, as the information must cross the corpus callosum (the thick band of nerve fibers that divides the cerebrum into left and right hemispheres). During the transfer, and when it crosses the corpus callosum, the information gets flipped. For example: *saw* becomes *was* and *b* is perceived as *d*. It is common for numerals to transpose when there is not a dominant eye. Reading, writing, spelling, and math all have serious consequences because of visual mixed dominance. When auditory information is inefficiently stored, the result is stuttering and a slow information-processing rate. As the brain goes searching for information that is not where it should be, the individual stutters. The stutter can be seen in speech as well as in writing. As you can imagine, the timing of information processing is significantly slower when either visual or auditory dominance has not been established. The time it takes for the brain to retrieve information varies from day to day. Just like the books and toys in the toy chest, sometimes you can find what you want, and sometimes you cannot.

Adding to the dilemma of inconsistent information recall is the fact that inappropriately stored information is kept in the sub-dominant hemisphere of the brain, where emotions reside and exercise unfathomable control. If any pressure or stress is added to a person's task, information will be nearly impossible to retrieve. It's like the feeling you get when someone you know is coming toward you and you don't recall her name, so you begin to panic as she approaches because you just can't remember. You struggle and grasp, but just cannot pull it to the forefront of your mind. Or, maybe in a discussion, you tried to think of the name of a movie or an actor in that movie, but for the life of you, you cannot come up with the information. Then, many hours later, while not even contemplating it, the names pop up from nowhere. The data is clearly there, but you just can't find it when needed.

Now, relate this memory problem to the student who studies and studies. He knows the information, and has it stored. However, when he takes the test, he freezes. He simply cannot recall the information. Inconsistent recall, especially when in a testing environment, is the single largest reason I detest the high use of testing in our culture. A test is not a reflection of what a person knows, but rather is a reflection of how well the person is able to access that information in a testing, and often stressful environment.

When a neurologically disorganized person is placed in stressful or testing situations, they go subdominant; meaning their emotions take over. In turn, this severely hampers or even denies them access to logical, analytical thought, reasoning, and memory. It is easy to become exasperated when you are the parent of a child with mixed dominance. Altering your voice, even just a little bit in frustration because your child knew a math process all week but then forgot it on Friday, can send that child into the sub-dominant world. At that point, reasoning will not do any good; apologizing will not do much good either until the sub-dominant deluge of emotions is gone and the child is back into the state where logic and reasoning can be accessed.

The issues that surface from mixed dominance have nothing to do with an individual's intelligence, diligence, will power, or determination. These issues are simply a by-product of the state of the central nervous system (CNS). The pathways have not been inputting into the brain accurately, so the output is haphazard and inconsistent.

Think of the CNS like a major highway. The eastbound lanes should have all the trucks and cars heading east, the westbound traffic should all be heading west. If every fourth or fifth car were reversed in direction, there would be chaos on that highway. Like this highway, the signals on the pathways to and from the brain cannot have correct "traffic flow" when they are not organized appropriately, and most often, chaos is the result.

We have many very bright children throughout our country who are struggling with learning. These children cannot seem to get it together. Studying is difficult; retrieval of information is inconsistent. Then, when you add mixed dominance to their problem, undoubtedly the most debilitating part of their neurological disorganization, the result is that they are living in their subdominant hemisphere all day long. These children can be moody, angry, and emotionally challenging. They can shut down emotionally, physically, or mentally; or they can become the class clown doing almost anything to mask an inability to keep up with the class. When these children go *subdominant*, all these negative symptoms become exacerbated. Their emotions are so out of control because they are living in the subdominant hemisphere, which is the source of emotional function, instead of in the dominant hemisphere where analytical thinking, reasoning, and logic reside. The subdominant hemisphere becomes their controlling hemisphere and prevents access to their dominant hemisphere.

It bears repeating, that when the subdominant hemisphere is in control, emotions are in control! Children experiencing this situation usually wear their feelings on their shirtsleeves, unless they learn to suppress them. Consequently, the children have meltdowns. It's during meltdowns when I typically see the best-intentioned parents try to reason with their children, thinking that the more they talk, the more their children will understand and change. In reality, when a person goes *subdominant*, it is as if a brick wall comes up. At this point, there is no reasoning. None!

If you have a child who goes subdominant, stop talking immediately and do something to pull them out of it, something like having them run around the house a couple of times, or do 20 jumping jacks. You must do something physical to pull them out of their subdominant hemisphere because there is no reasoning while they are there. The logical part – the reasoning part – of their brain is totally inaccessible to them during that time when they are sub-dominant. In order to prevent a shutdown situation, what is needed is to get them cortically dominant. This means properly aligning their eye, ear, hand, and foot. When the correct hemisphere is in control, then the person is capable of logic and reasoning.

Dyslexia is symptomatic of visual dominance not being achieved. As we discussed previously, when this occurs, the brain takes the visual information and stores it improperly in the wrong hemisphere. Then, when the person tries to retrieve the stored information, it is not where it should be. Naturally, the brain begins searching. Once found, the information must be deposited correctly into storage, which the brain begins to do. As the brain is transferring the information, it crosses the corpus callosum, and when that happens, as we said earlier, the information often flips: *spot* becomes *tops*; *p* becomes *q*. Such letter and word reversals reflect visual mixed dominance and are not something with which we have to live with or compensate for. We see the symptoms of dyslexia resolve in a person all the time, once dominance has been achieved.

As we mentioned previously, stuttering is symptomatic of mixed auditory dominance; the language center has not fully matured. A person should have only one language center and it should be in the opposite hemisphere of the dominant ear. A dominant ear has not been established when an individual is using either *both ears* or the *wrong ear* for the input of information to be stored. Stuttering and stammering often result because information is inefficiently stored and then, when a person tries to retrieve it, he or she cannot find it. As the brain attempts to find the necessary information, anything from mild stammering to severe stuttering results.

These symptomatic results of mixed dominance are entirely reversible. The learning disability labels do NOT have to be lifelong situations. All children with learning issues have low-processing and mixed dominance problems. **And all children with these issues can be helped by achieving correctly aligned dominance and improving their processing.**

My colleague and founder of Little Giant Steps and Brain Sprints, Jan Bedell Ph.D., conducted studies with children who had received the labels Dyslexia and ADD/ADHD. The results were sad but not surprising. The findings, which you can see in the following two charts, identify neurological disorganization as the root cause of learning issues. The charts reflect children currently locked into a life from which they can be set free when the NDApproach becomes more widely known and utilized.

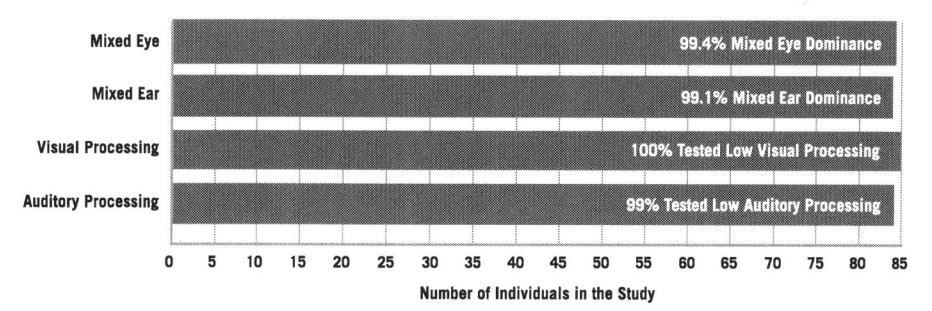

**NeuroDevelopmental Assessment Results in ADD / ADHD-labeled Children**

|  |  |
|---|---|
| Mixed Eye | 99.4% Mixed Eye Dominance |
| Mixed Ear | 99.1% Mixed Ear Dominance |
| Visual Processing | 100% Tested Low Visual Processing |
| Auditory Processing | 99% Tested Low Auditory Processing |

Number of Individuals in the Study

**NeuroDevelopmental Assessment Results in Dyslexic-labeled children**

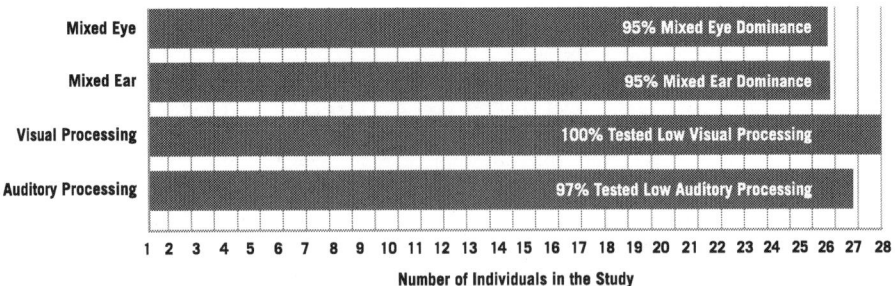

|  |  |
|---|---|
| Mixed Eye | 95% Mixed Eye Dominance |
| Mixed Ear | 95% Mixed Ear Dominance |
| Visual Processing | 100% Tested Low Visual Processing |
| Auditory Processing | 97% Tested Low Auditory Processing |

Number of Individuals in the Study: 1-28

Only after a person has received, processed, and stored information correctly can they continue successfully with **the 4th step** for learning – *utilizing the information.*

What I want you to understand is that learning has nothing to do with output; but output is where the focus is for most of the traditional means of education. You cannot generate good output without good input! The information must first be accurately received, then processed appropriately, and stored correctly. This all must be entered through the proper alignment, or correct dominance, that is written in the blueprint for each person. Instead of focusing on how to help our children by organizing their central nervous systems correctly, our culture's mode of operation is to identify, label and then devise strategies for coping and compensating for the life-long struggle that will surely ensue.

We say, "NO!" This does not have to be. As more and more children are falling behind, struggling to keep going and becoming more and more frustrated and discouraged, we want to shout loud and clear, "It doesn't have to be this way!" There is a better way! There is an escape for the life-long struggles so many are facing, and that way out is not by coping and compensating. The better way is through brain stimulation and the resulting neurological organization.

# Carter's Journey
*"Challenging Delays and NeuroDevelopment"*

*Hope And A Future* has been such a blessing to our family. Carter was in a special program for monitoring delays from birth because of his mother's hearing disability. At about 12 months, they started to notice delays in speech and fine motor skills. He was in speech therapy from the time he was a toddler until he was in fifth grade. He had extreme separation anxiety, which attributed to being informed that he was probably on the spectrum. While this wasn't a huge surprise, it was hard to accept because Carter had two autistic cousins, and we saw how things were handled differently with his cousins once a label was applied, and felt we wanted a different future for Carter.

We tried all kinds of alternative therapies, supplements, and diets. Some of them had some measure of success, and some of them didn't. We ended up pulling Carter out of junior high after 7th grade due to bullying.

We heard Linda speak at a homeschooling conference and decided to have Carter, who was sixteen at the time, evaluated by her. We found out he had mixed dominance, among other issues. We have seen significant improvement in Carter, and we absolutely believe the time and effort put into neurodevelopmental intervention is worth it. Carter used to have a very stiff way of walking, and he carried his hands by his shoulders. He now walks with a more normal carefree gait.

Our orthodontist wants to put Carter on his website because his facial structure has changed so much. I believe that much of that has to do with the facial activities Linda has us doing with him. Carter is having a much easier time with comprehension and application of schoolwork. I recently started an apologetics curriculum for him, and after looking at it thought we might be reaching but would give it a try. Not only is Carter comprehending it, but he can intelligently discuss it.

We are such believers in this program that we will have our daughters, who have no developmental issues, evaluated. I believe that most children could benefit in one way or another from doing neurodevelopmental work.

CHAPTER FOUR

# Eradicating Dyslexia!

*But when I looked again, they were gone!*
*When I searched for them, I could not find them!*
Psalms 37:36 – New Living Translation

Dyslexia is always rooted in mixed dominance and disorganization of the central nervous system. Dyslexia is simply neurological disorganization, which can be re-wired. It does not have to be the lifelong sentence of struggle most propose. We have the privilege of seeing the symptoms of dyslexia disappear all the time. Sadly, many parents receive a diagnosis of dyslexia for a child who struggles with reading and no hope is offered. It is common for these parents to hear that there is no cure for dyslexia. Incorrectly advised, parents are told that their child will always have dyslexia and that the only means of treatment are remedial education and/or engaging in coping and compensating measures. Dyslexia is not a disease, so it is true that there is no cure for this disease that doesn't exist. However, the truth of the matter is that dyslexia is diagnosed based on a list of symptoms. Through the identification of the root causes, those symptoms can then be targeted through specific stimulation to the brain, which decreases and even eradicates the symptoms. It is very simple.

Scientists and researchers differ in their estimations about the percentage of the population having dyslexia. Most current estimates are from 10 to 15 percent; it may even be upwards of 17 to 20 percent. Many people who are currently experiencing dyslexia symptoms are undiagnosed, making accurate estimation considerably more difficult.

Ida, a mom I worked with for many years, told a friend of hers about the NDApproach and how it had changed her son's life. Her friend, who was a doctor, was astounded by the progress of a child who had been diagnosed as medically fragile, with Down syndrome, and who was not walking or talking at seven years old. To learn that within four months of starting his ND program, Ida's son, Isaiah, was enjoying half-mile walks, was running, and was speaking in full sentences – which was incomprehensible to her. Ida's friend, Lynne, had never seen any transformation like that in all her experience. It is good to note that Lynne was a doctor three times over. She was a psychiatrist, a Ph.D., and a naturopathic doctor, so her experience was extensive. She wanted to meet me and learn more about the approach that could produce such results.

When we finally met a few months later, we discussed the NDApproach and its unique perspective on the challenges many individuals are facing, as well as how our method treats those challenges so differently from standard protocol. When I mentioned we see dyslexia go away all the time, Lynne shook her head in amazement and asked me if I realized that *NO ONE* says that, nor has these results. And Lynne was right; people do not see these kinds of results because they do not even believe they are possible to achieve; thus, expectations are lowered which has resulted in modifications becoming the standard practice.

We have worked with many children and adults who have received the diagnosis of dyslexia and have worked with many more who have the symptoms of dyslexia but have not gone through the formal diagnostic process. Whether officially diagnosed dyslexic or not, a person struggling with reading is in a very frustrating and seemingly hopeless situation. Through many years of working with these individuals who are struggling, one commonality has surfaced: they all presented with neurological disorganization. Many, but not all, were found to be using the wrong hand for dominance and were going against the grain of their genetic coding to which the body was to align. No one is talking about this anomaly outside of the NeuroDevelopmental Approach field. The thought of changing someone's *handedness* has been fiercely opposed by other professionals, who argue that this ABSOLUTELY should not be done. Yet, our experience has shown that this is an effective path and one that we desire to share with families so they can make treatment decisions for themselves.

## Lauren Scott's Story
*"What a blessing!"*

The Scott family has eight children and learning to read was never an issue for any of them until Lauren, their youngest. Lauren was diagnosed with dyslexia at age eight; the diagnosis reconfirmed when she was 11. The recommendations offered after the testing included accommodations, intervention, remediation, and private tutoring, which are typical recommendations. For seven years, Lauren worked through many of the available phonetic reading programs advertised to help with dyslexia. It was very slow, excruciatingly painful, and frustrating for Lauren. By the time Lauren was 12, she was reading at the sixth-grade level, with comprehension at high fifth grade. Some would think this was a success, given her diagnosis, but for Lauren, it was only one piece of the puzzle she lived with every day. Life was difficult; getting through each day was exhausting. Living with poor time management, minimal attention span, and extreme disorganization, it was understandable it took all her effort to get through each day. Lauren's mom, Julie, knew there had to be more going on and that those laborious phonetic programs weren't addressing Lauren's issues. Like so many determined moms, Julie never stopped seeking help for her daughter and happened upon the NDApproach in June 2013. Julie wrote about finding ND, *"Then we heard about a program that had its participants wearing an eye patch and other weird-sounding techniques. After talking with another mom who had seen great results with the NDApproach and hearing Linda's presentation, we decided to give it a try."* That is when everything began to change for the better for Lauren.

Lauren's first evaluation in July 2013 revealed a familiar pattern: a bright, engaging young person with a dyslexia diagnosis who had improperly aligned against the organizational blueprint for her body. Lauren's seven long years of struggle began when that blueprint surfaced, and she had chosen the wrong hand for dominance. Julie's goals and expectations for Lauren were, *"No more letter reversals, better processing and memorization, longer attention span, progress in spelling."*

**July 2013 1st Evaluation Notes**
Age: 12 years 2 months
Diagnosis: Dyslexia
6th grade complete: Homeschool University Model

Behavior and Concerns: Tends to be impatient and demanding on herself, attention span short, disorganized, time management issues, cyclical academics.

Crawl: Serialized cross pattern – complete
Creep: Cross pattern – complete, synchronization incomplete
Primitive Reflexes (tested) not integrated: Babinski, Moro

Auditory Digit Spans (ADS) . . . . . . . . . . . . . . . . .5, bridging 6
Auditory Conceptual Word Sequence (ACWS) . .4, bridging 5
Visual Digit Spans (VDS). . . . . . . . . . . . . . . . . . .6
Visual Flash Digits (VFD). . . . . . . . . . . . . . . . . .4-5

Math (1st ten minutes timed)  6th grade, 7th month (6.7)
Math (untimed) . . . . . . . . . . . . . . . . . . . . . . . . .7.1
Word Recognition. . . . . . . . . . . . . . . . . . . . . . . .6.6
Comprehension . . . . . . . . . . . . . . . . . . . . . . . . .5.8

Auditory Dominance . . . . . . . . . . . . . . . . . . . . . Mixed
Visual Dominance . . . . . . . . . . . . . . . . . . . . . . Right-Mixed
Manual Dominance . . . . . . . . . . . . . . . . . . . . Right
Foot Dominance . . . . . . . . . . . . . . . . . . . . . . . Left-Mixed

We had provided a program, which the family followed, and we were delighted to see at Lauren's second evaluation some significant changes for the better. She was adapting well to changing her hand dominance from the right to the left hand, which was fantastic to see. Her processing skills were increasing, as evidenced by her reading comprehension, which jumped more than three grade levels. Sometimes when you are working on re-aligning dominance, there can also be an increase in other problems. This was the case with Lauren, who experienced more word-skipping while reading and more jumbled-up letters. The family was faithful to continue with the updated Individualized NeuroDevelopmental Plan (INP) specifically designed for Lauren despite seeing some setbacks.

**November 2013 2nd Evaluation Notes**
Age: 12 years 6 months
Diagnosis: Dyslexia
7th grade: Homeschool University Model

Behavior and Concerns: Improved time management

Creep: Serialized cross pattern - complete
Primitive Reflexes (tested) not integrated: Babinski, Moro

ADS . . . . . . . . . . . . . 6
ACWS . . . . . . . . . . . 5
VDS . . . . . . . . . . . . 6-7
VFD . . . . . . . . . . . . 5, bridging 6

Math (timed) . . . . . . . 6.3
Math (untimed) . . . . . . 7.1
Word Recognition . . . . . 6.8
Comprehension . . . . . . 8.4

Auditory Dominance . . . . Mixed-Left
Visual Dominance . . . . . Right-Mixed
Manual Dominance . . . . Mixed-Left
Foot Dominance . . . . . . Left-Mixed

Lauren's third evaluation showed even more improvement and progress. Her hand change to the left was nearly complete; her writing was much more natural; and her pencil control steadier. The letter and number reversals that had always plagued her had significantly decreased. Her reading comprehension had increased again, this time by nearly two full grade levels. The most exciting news, though, was that for the first time in her life, Lauren was truly enjoying reading.

**March 2014 3rd Evaluation Notes**
Age: 12 years 10 months
Diagnosis: Dyslexia
7th grade: Homeschool University Model

Behavior and Concerns: Spelling is the only concern

Primitive Reflexes (tested) not integrated: Babinski
Moro complete

ADS . . . . . . . . . . . 6
ACWS . . . . . . . . . . 5-6
VDS . . . . . . . . . . . 6-7
VFD . . . . . . . . . . . 5, bridging 6

Math (timed) . . . . . . 6.3
Math (untimed) . . . . . 7.1
Word Recognition . . . . 7.7
Comprehension . . . . . 10.2

Auditory Dominance . . . Left-Mixed
Visual Dominance . . . . Right-Mixed
Manual Dominance . . . Left-Mixed
Foot Dominance . . . . . Left-Mixed

Dominance-shifting to the left was happening for Lauren and things were progressing nicely. By the time I saw her for the fourth evaluation, everything was starting to come together beautifully. She was no longer skipping words and lines while reading and the reversals were nearly gone. Lauren was reading for fun at higher grade levels! And finally, her math computation had an increase of more than two grades, with increased speed. Upon testing, Lauren's visual pathway for dominance had substantially connected left, and the left-hand dominance had finalized, obviously the reason for her academic success. It truly is amazing that when the dominance lines up, as Lauren's was nearly complete, everything else falls into place. Julie's comment about her daughter was quite touching. She beamed from ear to ear as she relayed how responsible and caring Lauren had become. What a difference in just a year! They would continue seeing positive results for many months to come.

**July 2014 4th Evaluation Notes**
Age: 13 years 2 months
Diagnosis: Dyslexia
7th grade complete: Homeschool University Model

Behavior and Concerns: Spelling. Responsible and caring!
Primitive Reflexes (tested) not integrated: None
Babinski complete

ADS . . . . . . . . . . . . . 6
ACWS . . . . . . . . . . . 5-6
VDS . . . . . . . . . . . . . 6
VFD . . . . . . . . . . . . . 5, bridging 6

Math (timed) . . . . . . . 7.4
Math (untimed) . . . . . . 9.5
Word Recognition . . . . . 7.9
Comprehension . . . . . . 10.2

Auditory Dominance . . . . Left
Visual Dominance . . . . . Left-Mixed
Manual Dominance . . . . Left
Foot Dominance . . . . . . Left

In November 2014, 16 months after starting an NDApproach program, Lauren's dominance transformation was complete. She had established left-side dominance and her parents no longer saw the struggles that had held her back and challenged her for years; math and reading levels continued to test at higher levels; and Julie had no academic, emotional, social, or behavioral concerns at all. Lauren was a sweet, caring, articulate, and kind young woman. Julie even laughed about how wonderful it was to see Lauren showing slight, yet age-appropriate mood swings. I just smiled, knowing those mood swings would have been more of a giant rollercoaster ride for the family had Lauren not aligned with her genetic blueprint of left-side dominance.

**November 2014 5th/Final Evaluation Notes**
Age: 13 years 6 months
Diagnosis: Dyslexia – Gone!
8th grade: Homeschool University Model

Behavior and Concerns: Better mental organization, information retention, and spelling improvements noted. No concerns.
Babinski complete

```
ADS . . . . . . . . . . . . .7
ACWS . . . . . . . . . . .5-6
VDS . . . . . . . . . . . . .7
VFD . . . . . . . . . . . . .7, bridging 8

Math (timed)    . . . . . . .7.7
Math (untimed) . . . . . .10.8
Word Recognition . . . . .8.3
Comprehension . . . . . .11.8

Auditory Dominance . . . . Left
Visual Dominance . . . . . Left
Manual Dominance . . . . Left
Foot Dominance . . . . . . Left
```

Lauren's dominance was re-evaluated in March 2015 and had successfully held 100 percent left.

In August 2017, Julie emailed an update, letting me know that Lauren would be off to college that upcoming weekend. She had finished her high school career at a local private academy along with the university-model school. Julie had been thrilled to report Lauren had kept up with the heavy reading she had to do and even successfully navigated the challenges of Spanish and memory work in the sciences. Julie thanked me for our part in Lauren's success, ending her note with, *"She did it!"*

While Lauren's exit from dyslexia came about by changing her dominant hand and aligning the eye, ear, and foot to match the appropriate side, a hand change is not always needed, as we relate in Kristen's story below.

## Kristen Oliver's Story
*"From Dyslexia to Doctor!"*

When I first met Kristen, she was a delightful 10-year-old whose smile and sparkling eyes filled the room with joy. She had a great attitude and was a very hard worker. Jessica, Kristen's mom, confided in me the concerns she was having about her daughter. School was a continual struggle for Kristen, despite just completing an intensive dyslexia correction program. Her grades were C's at best, despite the nightly hours of continual schoolwork review. Kristen was also picking scabs and little skin irritations until bloody and was finicky about what clothing she would wear. She was also overeating, indulging primarily with carbohydrates, sugar, and dairy. Jessica explained the poor diet as Kristen's way of handling the enormous stress she was under and all that was going on in her life. Her parents' divorce had been final for several years, but there were numerous custody challenges and court battles, leaving Kristen feeling uneasy and vulnerable. If this wasn't enough disruption, Kristen continually battled the relentless dyslexia cloud hanging over her. She never had a break from the daily exhaustion, extra work, and stress that it caused.

**May 2006 1st Evaluation Notes**
Age: 10 years 8 months
Diagnosis: Dyslexia
5th grade: Public School

1st Concerns: Pre-school
Behavior and Concerns: Had completed yet another dyslexia program and was still experiencing significant learning challenges and dyslexic struggles.

Crawl: Alternated cross and homolateral patterns – incomplete
Creep: Cross pattern – complete, synchronization incomplete
Primitive Reflexes (tested) none tested

```
ADS . . . . . . . . . . . 5
ACWS . . . . . . . . . . 5
VDS . . . . . . . . . . . 9
VFD . . . . . . . . . . . 6

Math . . . . . . . . . . 5.7
Word Recognition . . . . 9.7
Comprehension . . . . . 7.8

Auditory Dominance . . . Mixed
Visual Dominance . . . . Right-Mixed
Manual Dominance . . . Right
Foot Dominance . . . . . Left-Mixed
```

Kristen switched schools for sixth grade and attended a stringent parochial school. New friends, new teachers, new expectations and goals abounded. Despite the high stress and demands both Jessica and her daughter faced, they were very faithful to the INP that I had designed specifically for Kristen. They were thrilled to see Kristen's reading word recognition and comprehension test two years higher at her first re-evaluation. Kristen was seeing notable changes in how she was handling situations and disappointments, most likely due to her auditory processing ability going from that of a five-year-old to within normal limits.

Kristen had added playing school volleyball into her extremely tight schedule, which added two-three hours, three times a week, to her schedule. Participating in volleyball was good for Kristen as an avenue of success and it bolstered her confidence in her abilities. Something needed to give, though, so it was my recommendation that Jessica inquire with Kristen's teachers about getting her homework reduced substantially, better yet, having it eliminated. After volleyball and her nightly two hours of homework, there was little time for her INP, which needed to be a high priority.

The reality was, Kristen doing an NDApproach program would be a season in her life. That season would be a temporary period that would correct the underlying root causes of her issues, producing life-long positive changes. Kristen was doing too much, which was lowering the overall intensity and effectiveness of everything she was doing.

**September 2006 2nd Evaluation Notes**
Age: 11 years 1 month
Diagnosis: Dyslexia
6th grade: Parochial School

Behavior and Concerns: Good attitude! Handling hurts better. She can now laugh at her mistakes rather than pouting.

Crawl: Improved synchronization – incomplete. Intermittent homolateral crawl
Creep: Cross pattern – complete, synchronization incomplete

ADS . . . . . . . . . . .6
ACWS . . . . . . . . . .5
VDS . . . . . . . . . . .6-7
VFD . . . . . . . . . . .5, bridging 6

Math . . . . . . . . . .5.2
Word Recognition . . . .11.7
Comprehension . . . . .9.5

Auditory Dominance . . . Mixed-Right
Visual Dominance . . . . Right
Manual Dominance . . . Right
Foot Dominance . . . . . Right-Mixed

Jessica couldn't wait to tell me that Kristen's grades were all A-C's at her third evaluation. She was thrilled that her daughter was listening and understanding significantly better. Kristen had begun expressing her thoughts at a higher level, even asking questions when she was confused about a current discussion. These were all excellent signs that her neurological organization was progressing. There were a few new behavioral concerns which had surfaced, which is not unusual to see when re-organizing the central nervous system, and likely were temporary symptoms of the re-wiring Kristen was experiencing.

**February 2007 3rd Evaluation Notes**
Age: 11 years 6 months
Diagnosis: Dyslexia
6th grade: Parochial School

Behavior and Concerns: Clinging to mom, wanting excessive hugs. Teasing, not respecting boundaries noted.

Crawl: Improved synchronization – incomplete. Intermittent homolateral
Creep: Serialized cross pattern – complete
Primitive Reflexes (tested) not integrated: Moro

```
ADS . . . . . . . . . . . .7
ACWS . . . . . . . . . .5
VDS . . . . . . . . . . .8
VFD . . . . . . . . . . .7-8

Math . . . . . . . . . .5.7
Word Recognition . . . .12.9
Comprehension . . . . .10.2

Auditory Dominance. . . .Mixed-Right
Visual Dominance . . . .Right
Manual Dominance . . .Right
Foot Dominance. . . . .Left-Mixed
```

School was continuing to go well for Kristen. Her grades maintained the A-C range she had achieved. Her math score jumped nearly two grade levels at her fourth evaluation testing, and her word recognition advanced almost a year. It was time to transition the word recognition testing to Level 2, and we anticipated the grade dropping with the difference in the scoring measure. Finally, we were seeing success with the auditory dominance shifting to the right side. Sometimes it takes a while for the pathways to develop and expand. Kristen's processing skills continued to increase and were at accelerated levels. Sound sensitivity, which had always been an issue for Kristen, was no longer being experienced. While Kristen had been doing the Suzuki method with the violin and piano since she was young, Jessica noted a substantial improvement in her musical abilities. Kristen suddenly began playing music by ear, as well as reading musical notes, which had always been difficult. She had a stronger grasp with the violin bow and had started playing piano with both hands. To Jessica's relief, she happily reported that Kristen was now having many more good days than bad ones.

**May 2007 4th Evaluation Notes**
Age: 11 years 9 months
Diagnosis: Dyslexia
6th grade: Parochial School

Behavior and Concerns: Decreased clingy behavior, less need for hugs

Crawl: Serialized cross pattern – complete
Primitive Reflexes (tested) not integrated: Moro

| | |
|---|---|
| ADS | 8 |
| ACWS | 6 |
| VDS | 8 |
| VFD | 9 |
| | |
| Math | 7.5 |
| Word Recognition (Level 1) | 13.7 |
| Word Recognition (Level 2) | 11.9 |
| Comprehension | 10.4 |
| | |
| Auditory Dominance | Right-Mixed |
| Visual Dominance | Right |
| Manual Dominance | Right |
| Foot Dominance | Left-Mixed |

There was an exciting change noted at Kristen's fifth evaluation. The very nasty habit of biting her fingers and fingernails that had plagued Kristen as long as her mother could remember had decreased significantly. Her math test scores were all A+, and Kristen was finally able to stay on a task until it was completed. Jessica reported Kristen was playing better with others and not taking out any frustration on anyone else, as she had in the past.

**September 2007 5th Evaluation Notes**
Age: 12 years 1 months
Diagnosis: Dyslexia
7th grade: Parochial School

Behavior and Concerns: Following directions improved, perseverance improved, decreased frustration

Primitive Reflexes (tested) not integrated: Moro

```
ADS . . . . . . . . . . . 8
ACWS . . . . . . . . . . 6
VDS . . . . . . . . . . . 9
VFD . . . . . . . . . . . 8
Math . . . . . . . . . . 6.7
Word Recognition . . . . 12.4
Comprehension . . . . . 11.4

Auditory Dominance. . . Right
Visual Dominance . . . . Right
Manual Dominance . . . Right
Foot Dominance . . . . . Right-Mixed
```

Achieving this kind of cortical hemispheric neurological organization is an incredible goal for an individual. For some, the road can be longer due to varying life factors. For Kristen, being in a private school, playing musical instruments, and taking part in sports limited the amount of program that realistically was achievable. Both Kristen and her mother were happy with the slower track for their journey. Their perseverance and patience were worth the time and effort it took. By the time I saw Kristen for her 6th evaluation, her dominance had fully established right-sided. Jessica was amazed at how far-reaching the changes in Kristen were. Learning issues were a thing of the past – even being able to do math mentally for the first time! Jessica commented that Kristen, who never wore jeans due to their discomfort, had now started wearing them. She laughed about how her daughter, who could never dribble a basketball, was now dribbling with great ease. Kristen's processing ability had diminished this evaluation, which could be explained by the increase in the continued tug-of-war regarding custody. Kristen hadn't lost the ability her increased processing afforded her; she was simply not able to do the drill as well due to the current stress.

### February 2008 6th Evaluation Notes
Age: 12 years 6 months
Diagnosis: Dyslexia – asymptomatic
7th grade: Parochial School

Behavior and Concerns: Quicker with work, fatigue, and stress issues noted with current custody/placement trials.
Primitive Reflexes (tested) not integrated: Moro

ADS . . . . . . . . . . . . 6-7
ACWS . . . . . . . . . . 5
VDS . . . . . . . . . . . 9
VFD . . . . . . . . . . . 6-7

Math . . . . . . . . . . 6.7
Word Recognition . . . . 13.0
Comprehension . . . . . 10.0

Auditory Dominance . . . Right
Visual Dominance . . . . Right
Manual Dominance . . . Right
Foot Dominance . . . . . Right

June 2008, we saw that magical, bitter-sweet evaluation for Kristen: her final one. We looked back on her initial assessment and had to laugh. Somewhere along the journey, Kristen had stopped picking her skin until it bled; the habit had simply disappeared, and we hadn't even realized it or remembered. It is common to entirely forget an issue that has resolved, which makes looking back and comparing *now vs then* quite exciting. With Kristen achieving full right-side dominance, her processing skills superior, and no evidence of dyslexia symptoms, I knew her life was going to be dramatically better for having done an NDApproach program. The plan was to have a final evaluation in June to ensure the reorganization was solidly in place.

### June 2008 7th/Final Evaluation Notes
Age: 12 years 10 months
Diagnosis: Dyslexia – Gone!
7th grade complete: Parochial School

Behavior and Concerns: No concerns
Primitive Reflexes (tested) not integrated: Moro (suspect not integrating due to continual family stress)

ADS . . . . . . . . . . . 8
ACWS . . . . . . . . . . 6
VDS . . . . . . . . . . . 9
VFD . . . . . . . . . . . 8

Math . . . . . . . . . . 6.5
Word Recognition . . . . 12.4
Comprehension . . . . . 11.4

| | |
|---|---|
| Auditory Dominance... | Right |
| Visual Dominance.... | Right |
| Manual Dominance... | Right |
| Foot Dominance..... | Right |

Years later, when Kristen was 21 years old, I received an email that just made my heart smile. The most rewarding part of what we do is also the hardest: saying goodbye and letting them fly. So, when a parent comes back years later to give us updates on their child, it is the absolute best and reinforces why we do what we do.

> *"I have recommended your program to many parents and hope they have as much success as my daughter has.*
>
> *You might like to know my daughter was a student of yours about ten years ago. The exercises were daunting at first, but after several months she noticed the differences in her life.*
>
> *Fast forward to today. My precious daughter is now a happy, healthy 21-year-old in her first year of Chiropractic College. The Lord has blessed us in so many ways!*
>
> *I attribute her success in life to the patience and teachings of nutrition and brain exercises from you. Now that she has matured past the teenage years (think bad food choices and her "Aah Mom, why can't we eat like other people??" comments), Kristen is embracing the healthy lifestyle opportunities on her campus.*
>
> *So, may I say again a heartfelt, "Thank You," for the hope you gave us and the blessings I hope will pass to future generations! May God continue to bless your efforts!"*

And then a few years later, when Kristen graduated as a chiropractor, this marvelous note came in from Jessica.

> *"Keep Going! You ARE making a difference in many lives. Just think, from dyslexic to doctor in record time after completing the program!"*

Achieving neurological organization is imperative for eliminating the root causes of challenges. Once obtained, the newly established brain organization typically locks-in and maintains this pathway system. Occasionally, something will happen, and the dominance will revert, not holding the new dominant pathways. The family always knows, though, that something has gone wrong. That is what happened with Jason Sanders. Anita, Jason's mom, knew he just wasn't at his peak performance and wanted me to re-evaluate him to see if I could discern what had gone amiss. It had been a little more than four years since Jason had graduated from his ND program. Jason was just days away from his 17th birthday and was a confident, articulate, strapping football player.

What a contrast I saw from his first evaluation when he was 11 years old. At 11, Jason was short-tempered, impatient, impulsive, forgetful, and diagnosed dyslexic. His parents' first concerns surfaced when he was five years old because Jason had been unable to learn letters. As he got older, difficulties with reading, spelling, and completing instructions surfaced. When I first saw him in November 2013, Jason had a left-dominant blueprint but was using his right hand as the dominant hand with all sports. He was experiencing letter reversals, left/right confusion, and mirror-writing. Jason was mostly left-foot dominant, but his auditory dominance had incorrectly aligned to the right side. There was no doubt that his many learning issues were due to his severe mixed dominance. Compounding these problems, coping and compensating were difficult because Jason's processing abilities were at a 4-5 year-old level. He also had several primitive reflexes that had not integrated. Eagerly, the Sanders family went home to start Jason's ND program.

Twenty months later, Jason graduated completely left-side dominant. His processing increased to levels appropriate for his age, and the primitive reflexes had correctly integrated. Jason was no longer having any learning challenges or dyslexic symptoms. Anita commented that he was confident, relaxed, at ease in any situation, and happy!

Now, four years later, in August 2019, Jason still maintained a confident, happy, relaxed demeanor. Anita said that there was something just *off* from the full progress he had achieved. Moms are usually correct, and this was the case with Anita. Jason's dominant left ear had weakened, and he was again using his right ear part of the time for inputting information for storage. His neurological organization was no longer complete. While discussing what may have happened, Anita divulged what I believe was the culprit. Jason had done a lot of swimming on a competitive team that summer. I have seen auditory dominance shift when one ear has fluid retention and the opposite ear does not. It was entirely plausible there could have been retained water in the left ear canal, and the brain adjusted back to the old pathway for more efficiency when necessary.

Before leaving that afternoon, Jason looked at me and said, "*I thought you were crazy when I was 11 years old and you told me I had to use my left hand for everything. I thought you were absolutely nuts!*" Then he continued, "*But, it was the best thing I have ever done. All my struggles with school disappeared. I even lost the dyslexia label! Next week I start looking at colleges for next year. I don't think I would have been able to go to college if I had not done an ND program.*" I was so proud of Jason and what a delight to have heard his perspective. I imagine there are quite a few people who have had very similar thoughts regarding my recommended hand changes.

**Dyslexia can and does go away!**

## My Own Story

The road to neurological organization is definitely an interesting one, filled with struggles and hard work. It also can be very revealing about who the real person – the one underneath all the disorder – truly is. The end discovery is so worth the time and effort that must be put in to doing the NDApproach.

Dyslexic was probably the label that I would have received, had labeling been "popular" at the time I was in school. I had all kinds of learning issues and even though I did well, it took a lot of work to get there. For the most part, I was a good student, although I never liked school. In all honesty, I hated school. Some subjects, like geometry and chemistry, were just ridiculously hard. Other subjects, like German, were impossible. Despite my terrible first year of high school (when the math teacher told my mother I was absent more than I was present) I worked extra hard and was able to finish my senior year early. I could not wait to be finished with school. It was a major celebration day when I left that institution and I never looked back. In fact, I did not even return for the graduation ceremonies, my diploma was sent to me in the mail.

My sisters were both avid readers, but unlike them, I never enjoyed reading. My sisters excitedly left for college, but to my parents' great disappointment, I refused to even think of it. My decision not to go had nothing to do with intelligence but it had everything to do with my learning struggles and my feeling that there was no way I could manage college.

Less than a year after graduation, I married Lee. I loved Lee and he loved me, so getting married was the happiest day of my life. Setting up our household was another thing. When you are disorganized on the inside, your life usually reflects it and will be disorganized on the outside, and I was no exception. I was an extremely disorganized person and it showed in every area of my life.

My disorganization showed in many ways. I had five or six "junk" drawers in my kitchen. The laundry got done every week; however, it never got folded and put away – we just picked what we needed from the laundry basket that was never empty. There were stacks and piles of papers in several locations throughout the house and whenever I needed something, I would shuffle painfully through papers and go through nearly every stack before finding what I wanted. My kitchen countertops looked more like tables at a garage sale – there was no hope of chopping anything on them until mass clean-up took place. Every closet in our home was a disaster. Our daily hope was that nothing would fall out when we opened the doors. Even our floors were covered with things tossed about – there was clutter everywhere. Preparing for company took days of cleaning and living this way went on for years.

After children came into our lives, I would be emotionally and physically "done" by 6:00 or 7:00 at night. Dinner was over, dishes were washed, and I was checking out for the night. I would look over at Lee to signal that he was "on." If the boys needed something, they would have to go to Dad because I was physically and emotionally drained. I did not know it at the time, but it takes an incredible amount of energy to be neurologically disorganized.

I reached a point where I could not take this lifestyle any longer. My struggles from school had just transferred to struggles I was having as a wife and mother. By this time, we had learned about and had gotten our son, Scott on a neurodevelopmental program, I was in the midst of eight years of training in the neurodevelopmental field, and I thoroughly understood about neurological organization. With the realization that both my eye and ear were right-side dominant but that I was wired to be a left-handed person, I decided there was no choice but to change my own eye and ear to be left-side-dominant and to become organized.

As my dominance came in, I was amazed. One night, I realized that at ten o'clock I was still doing laundry. The difference in my energy level was incredible! Before my dominance came in, I could not make decisions. For example, one time I was in Oklahoma doing evaluations and it had been a long day and I was trying to determine where to eat. I thought of one restaurant but quickly dismissed it as too loud. Another restaurant was too expensive. I considered just buying something to eat from the grocery store and taking it back to the hotel, but that seemed like too much effort. In the end, I went back to my room without having dinner because I simply could not make a decision! The times when Lee asked where I wanted to eat out, my response was always the same – he should decide. After my dominance came in, he asked the same question and I told him where I wanted to go. He was incredulous as I had never decided before! We realized that he had only asked out of courtesy, not because he expected an answer!

Once I became neurologically organized, I found I was calmer and more rational. Previously, when someone said something that hurt my feelings, tears often welled up in my eyes. Once I became left-side-dominant, I heard these same comments not as criticism or attack, but rationally and with understanding. They had no real effect on my emotions! Some days I got busy and missed patching my eye and plugging my ear (activities for correcting dominance) and my son would ask if I had been occluding lately. I realized that on these days I was snapping at the kids a little more and was a bit crankier than I should have been which was what tipped him off. Mixed dominance has much more to do with emotionality and behavior than it does with personality. Being neurologically organized makes a huge difference in parenting, being a wife, and feeling more at peace.

As I became left-side dominant, all the clutter in my life slowly disappeared without my even being aware of it. One day I realized that the junk drawers were organized. I did not put any thought or effort into it, it just happened. The piles and clutter disappeared, and the closets became clean. When I did the program with Scott, I had everything we needed in a big basket. It had taken twice as long to do his program because I was continually searching through the basket for what I wanted. One day I realized that everything was in order – I no longer searched haphazardly through the basket. Instead, I had file boxes and envelopes, and everything was in its place. There was now a peace within me that I had never experienced before. What an amazing transformation! It took a year of work to successfully transfer dominance to my left side.

And then one day, much to my distress, everything returned. The clutter, the junk drawers, the inability to make decisions, the letter reversals and transposition of numbers, the fatigue, and even the emotionality. It had all crept back in and it hit me like a ton of bricks. Upon investigation, my eye dominance had not held firmly and that had put me back to living in a neurologically disorganized world. It was awful – even worse than before, for now I knew what it felt like to live life organized. I began to occlude (patch) my eye again and things restored back to calm and peace. Then, this abysmal experience happened once more. I could not understand it; my eye dominance simply would not hold. In order to maintain neurological dominance, I had to occlude my eye on a daily basis.

Several years later, our neurodevelopmental team was training a group to evaluate learning issues. At one point the group was practicing assessing eye inefficiencies and a woman who was evaluating my eyes loudly sucked in her breath and looked shocked. "Oh my!" was all she could muster up to say. Her reaction caused another person to examine me, with the same result. Finally, the lead neurodevelopmentalist evaluated my eyes. As it turns out, I had a severe divergent strabismus in my left eye. What this meant is that as my eyes were fixed on an object that was coming towards the bridge of my nose, the right eye continued to cross inward as it should, but my left eye diverged away from the nose. No wonder my visual dominance did not hold! The brain will not choose an inefficient pathway to be the primary pathway. Although I was an excellent reader, it was no wonder I never liked reading – it was too much work for my eyes to follow printed words, so reading was never enjoyable. This strabismus also explained the headaches I regularly experienced.

Had I had a neurodevelopmental evaluation, rather than diagnosing it on my own, this would have been caught much earlier and would have saved me much trouble. However, the experience of coming in and out of dominance has been quite insightful and has considerably expanded my knowledge for dominance-changing. Once the strabismus was decreased, my eye was stronger and was able to maintain dominance. As an added bonus, the headaches have disappeared, and I now love reading! What a difference aligning my dominance and properly storing information has made in my own life!

CHAPTER FIVE

# Eradicating ADD and ADHD

*You will look around for those brutal enemies,
but you won't find them because they are gone.*
Isaiah 41:12 – Contemporary English Version

I remember helping a friend who was going through a divorce. She had two children, and I was happy to watch them for her anytime she needed me. John, a quiet young boy at six, was glad to play contentedly by himself. Kelly, who was four, was an entirely different story. She could arrive at my front door, go through the living room, into the kitchen, and end up in the family room in less than five minutes. During that short time, Kelly turned my neat and orderly house into a total shamble. Toys, puzzles, blankets, pots, and pans would all be out everywhere. Chairs were overturned, lamps on the brink of falling, and rugs would be out of place. She was like a tornado shedding debris, whose path spared nothing. Kelly was my introduction to what living with attention deficit hyperactivity disorder could entail. Oh, my goodness! My heart went out to parents who live with that commotion all day long. After Kelly and her brother left, my head was still spinning.

Many times we see the problems of extreme hyperactivity and attention issues stemming from neurological organization incorrectly aligned. The only way to improve the situation is to create a one-sided laterality on the side that matches the blueprint of the genetic coding. What this means is making sure dominance of the ear, eye, and foot matches with the designated dominant hand for each individual. Quite often, as we recounted in the previous chapter, we see such struggles compounded because an individual uses the incorrect hand as the dominant hand. In this circumstance, it is essential to change that person's hand dominance. Changing "handedness" is a radical undertaking and is done only after much thought and analysis. When I started in this work nearly 30 years ago, we saw few individuals who were using the wrong hand for dominance. Either we were missing it early on or our culture has changed the structure of development in the past few decades, and it appears the latter may indeed be the case. Our culture emphasizes less gross motor movement during the critically important early developmental years, substituting fine-motor activities instead. Thirty years ago, we were not expecting a two-year-old to sit in preschool and do activities that promoted choosing hand dominance prematurely. Natural developmental stages, as discussed previously, have been usurped, and as a result, we have fundamentally changed the course of neurological development.

For many years, my advice to parents was to hand everything to their children midline, whether it was crayons, pencils, or eating utensils, with the thought of letting the child decide which side he or she would use – and not encourage the use of one hand over the other. That is no longer my advice. For the past fifteen years, I have been advising parents that if their child favors a particular hand before the age of five, the child must use the opposite hand as well. Before the age of five, it is unlikely that the genetic coding for dominance has established and we do not want the child making muscle memory on what could be the wrong side. If a child is still going back and forth, not deciding upon a hand, it is critically important not to make them choose – and not to choose a hand for them. It is far better to make sure they are doing some combat-style crawling and hands-and-knees creeping every day to ensure the lower levels of the brain are organized enough for the genetic coding regarding dominance to surface.

When handedness changes are deemed necessary, the shift from right-side to left-side dominance is noted significantly more than from left to right. That's understandable in a world where things tend to be set up for right-handedness. Most children are assumed right-handed until proven differently. I have had my share of left to right-side switches, though. Each individual is unique, and we want to align them to the correct side for them. Logan Travis is one person whose life completely changed through a left-hand transition.

## Logan Travis' Story
*"Incredibly hyperactive" to "No hyperactivity at all!"*

Derenda, a neurodevelopmentalist I had trained, called me with great concern regarding a highly active six-year-old she had just evaluated. We talked through her results and I designed a neurodevelopmental program for the child. Logan was the most hyperactive child Derenda had ever encountered, and she thought it would be best to transfer him to my caseload. There was a lot at stake for this precious boy. The school was insisting that the family put Logan on medication to control his hyperactivity and thus make him more "manageable" in the classroom. You cannot blame the teacher for being ill-equipped to handle children who don't fit into the mold of a seven-hour school day in a class of 30 children. Logan, who was on an IEP (Individualized Educational Plan) was failing in this system, and the school was adamant he could only remain by taking medication for ADHD. Determined to help their son stay off medication, Logan's parents, Gene and Donna, turned to the NDApproach for help, having witnessed the positive results it was having with their nephew who was having significant sensory issues.

Logan's initial evaluation in March 2011 revealed a unique set of circumstances interfering with his development. While Logan was a right-handed boy, his natural side appeared to be left. He reached for things left-handed; he turned pages entirely left-handed; his eye was 100 percent left-dominant; his ear was 80 percent left-dominant; and the unskilled tasks for his foot dominance (hopping, standing) were both left-dominant. Only kicking – a learned skill – was right-dominant. Curiously, the comments on their history form indicated Gary and Donna's concerns first emerged when Logan was two-three years old and had fractured his left arm three different times. With the left arm broken, the right became the primary arm of use, developing muscle memory for what appeared to have been the wrong side for dominance.

### March 2011 1st Evaluation Notes
Age: 6 years 7 months
Diagnosis: ADHD
1st grade: Public School – The school reports anxiety, visual perception/closure concerns, and the highest area of weakness is sensory processing.

Behavior and Concerns: Overly sensitive, cries easily. Temper tantrums often. Rigid, inflexible, and maturity concerns. Fully aware of the struggles, fragile self-esteem. Methodical, will breakdown, become mad or tearful if pushed too hard. Focus and attention span very limited. Cooperative, easy-going, sweet-natured.

Crawl: Challenging to do – incomplete
Creep: Incomplete
Primitive Reflexes (tested) not integrated: Babinski, Moro

```
ADS . . . . . . . . . . .4
ACWS . . . . . . . . .4
VDS . . . . . . . . . .5
VFD . . . . . . . . . .4

Math . . . . . . . . . .2.4
Word Recognition . . . .2.4
Comprehension . . . . .2.2
```

Auditory Dominance . . . Left-Mixed
Visual Dominance . . . . Left
Manual Dominance . . . Right-Mixed
Foot Dominance . . . . . Left-Mixed

We designed a program to begin working through the issues Logan was experiencing. The plan focused on organizing the central nervous system's lower levels, work on sensory dysfunction, and switch dominance to the left side –which appeared to be the actual blueprint for Logan. Gene and Donna were excited at the prospect of getting to the root of Logan's hyperactivity and inability to participate appropriately in his classroom or at home.

Four months later, Logan and his parents returned for their first re-evaluation. Even though they had been unable to start working on the hand-dominance switch, they had seen promising changes already. Gene and Donna reported a decrease in Logan's rigidity and inflexibility. He was less sensitive to touch, even tolerating Band-Aids, and he had fewer overreactions. Logan's sensitivity to loud sound was now minimal and his parents also noted an increase in his maturity.

**July 2011 2nd Evaluation Notes**
Age: 6 years 10 months
Diagnosis: ADHD
2nd grade: Public School

Behavior and Concerns: Methodical with tasks. Overreactions and rigidity decreased.

Crawl: Incomplete, went homolateral
Creep: Serialized cross pattern – complete
Primitive Reflexes (tested) not integrated: Babinski, Moro

ADS . . . . . . . . . . . 4
ACWS . . . . . . . . . . 4
VDS . . . . . . . . . . . 5
VFD . . . . . . . . . . . 4

Math . . . . . . . . . . 2.4
Word Recognition . . . . 2.4
Comprehension . . . . . 2.2

Auditory Dominance . . . Left-Mixed
Visual Dominance . . . . Left
Manual Dominance . . . Right-Mixed
Foot Dominance . . . . . Left-Mixed

The Travis family realized they would need the help and support of the school regarding the hand change, after all, Logan was in school the majority of his day. So, Gene and Donna called the school requesting an ARD (Admission, Review and Dismissal) meeting to get the left-hand switch included in Logan's IEP (Individualized Educational Plan). The ARD team included Logan's special education teacher, his classroom teacher, the head of the special education department, and the occupational therapist (OT) who worked with Logan. Everyone agreed to help Logan with this change except the OT. She vehemently disagreed with this decision and would not have any part in what she called an absolute mistake to change a child's handedness. The rest of the team agreed to proceed, and the OT decided to work with Logan's hand strength bilaterally.

Towards the end of October 2011, I had the privilege of evaluating Logan once again. It is crucial to the success of a neurodevelopmental program to be consistent with monitoring the program through re-evaluations. Gene and Donna were delighted with Logan's progress. Donna talked excitedly about how well Logan was doing, and she knew it was all due to this ND program. Her certainty that the plan was working came from experience because there had been a drastic reduction in his program activities during the previous two weeks and there had been corresponding regressions in Logan's behavior. Except for those two weeks, Logan had a great attitude; he was putting forth considerably more effort in his work and was doing very well with his peers. Donna was even amazed to report Logan's sound sensitivity had disappeared entirely!

**October 2011 3rd Evaluation Notes**
Age: 7 years 1 month
Diagnosis: ADHD
2nd grade: Public School

Behavior and Concerns: Has poor memory, lack of time management, and inability to work independently.

Crawl: Cross pattern and synchronization improved – incomplete
Primitive Reflexes (tested) not integrated: Babinski, Moro

ADS . . . . . . . . . . . 5
ACWS . . . . . . . . . . 5
VDS . . . . . . . . . . . 5
VFD . . . . . . . . . . . 4-5

Math . . . . . . . . . . 2.4
Word Recognition . . . . 4.7
Comprehension . . . . . 4.4

Auditory Dominance . . . Left-Mixed
Visual Dominance . . . . Left
Manual Dominance . . . Mixed-Left
Foot Dominance . . . . . Left-Mixed

Logan's next evaluation came in February of the following year, and the Travis family was concerned at that time that Logan was showing regressions. I quickly informed them that Logan was right on track, as this was a typical stage in the reorganizational process. At times during the reorganization of the central nervous system, pathways become "unplugged" to reroute and "re-plug" into the system. During this stage of restructuring, we often see some of the past emotionality and negative behaviors resurface almost out of nowhere. Logan was again having emotional outbursts, overreactions, mood changes, and rigidity. He had become increasingly defiant with his parents and schoolwork was overwhelming him. While this stage of reorganization can be challenging to go through, I encouraged his family not to panic and to keep going. What Logan was experiencing was temporary, and would pass, I counseled them. I had seen this too often, and knew they had to stay on course and move forward. Thankfully, Gene and Donna had the end-goal in sight, and they were determined to keep Logan going with his transformation to left-side dominance.

**February 2012 4th Evaluation Notes**
Age: 7 years 5 months
Diagnosis: ADHD
2nd grade: Public School

Behavior and Concerns: School is overwhelming! Increased outbursts, emotionality, rigidity, and mood swings.

Crawl: Serialize cross pattern – complete
Primitive Reflexes (tested) not integrated: Babinski, Moro

ADS . . . . . . . . . . . 5
ACWS . . . . . . . . . . 5
VDS . . . . . . . . . . . 5-6
VFD . . . . . . . . . . . 4-5

Math . . . . . . . . . . 2.2
Word Recognition . . . . 3.8
Comprehension . . . . . 4.4

Auditory Dominance . . . Left-Mixed
Visual Dominance . . . . Left
Manual Dominance . . . Mixed
Foot Dominance . . . . . Mixed-Left

A few months later, the June evaluation offered a clearer picture and showed that my predictions had come true. Logan was in a much better place in every area of his life. For example, there was a significant decrease in emotionality and irrationality; the few episodes Logan's behavior escalated were short-lived, and quicker for him to regulate. He was doing well socially, academically, and was "sharper" all-around according to his parents. Logan was displaying a substantial increase in maturity and was now doing much better in school. While I was not noting processing improvements during the evaluation testing, his parents were recording a 1-2 year processing gain at home. Occasionally we see this when a child doesn't test to their capability at the evaluation. Logan's functional processing abilities assured me his processing had indeed gone up. Test results for reading word recognition and comprehension continued to show good improvement. The most exciting news Gene and Donna shared was that Logan was now exclusively using his left hand for dominant function. He had made the switch, and the left-dominance switch was nearly complete!

### June 2012 5th Evaluation Notes
Age: 7 years 9 months
Diagnosis: ADHD
2nd grade complete: Public School

Behavior and Concerns: Improvement noted in all areas.

Cross pattern creep: Feet elevated – incomplete
Primitive Reflexes (tested) not integrated: Moro.
Babinski Complete

ADS . . . . . . . . . . . 5
ACWS . . . . . . . . . . 4-5
VDS . . . . . . . . . . . 5, bridged 6
VFD . . . . . . . . . . . 5, bridged 6

Math . . . . . . . . . . 2.4
Word Recognition . . . . 4.7
Comprehension . . . . . 4.4

Auditory Dominance . . . Left
Visual Dominance . . . . Left
Manual Dominance . . . Left
Foot Dominance . . . . . Left-Mixed

The October evaluation was bittersweet for me because it was Logan's last evaluation with *Hope And A Future*. Ultimately, this is the goal to see the child doing incredibly well, fully equipped to successfully go on without our assistance. It is a happy, yet sad day for us when we say goodbye to a family we have come to love. Gene and Donna reported Logan was doing remarkably at home and school. He was doing great socially and had an excellent attitude. They reported that they had absolutely no concerns behaviorally, emotionally, socially, or academically. His flexibility and cooperation were great. Logan was getting along exceptionally well with his sister – a huge side benefit they loved watching. They shared what a pleasure it was that the overreactions no longer controlled him. Gene and Donna couldn't be happier, and the school was amazed at the changes in Logan. Though there were a few things that still needed work for completing his neurological organization, Logan was indeed ready to graduate from his NDApproach program.

Donna, overwhelmed with joy, shared with me that Logan no longer needed the support of special education. The family had attended what became Logan's final IEP meeting just a few days previously. The IEP team was thrilled as they signed him out of special education, stating they had never seen such a transformation in a student. It was incredible for them to witness an extremely hyperactive young boy now without any hyperactivity; for someone with ADHD to no longer meet the criteria for an ADHD diagnosis. As Donna was leaving the IEP meeting, the occupational therapist followed to apologize privately for being so adamantly opposed to changing Logan's hand dominance. She didn't know why this process had worked for Logan but changing Logan's hand dominance had been needed.

The school had wanted Logan on medication to control his behavior and extreme hyperactivity; thankfully Logan's family had known about the neurodevelopmental approach to organizing the central nervous system – because of Logan's cousin, who was experiencing success working with *Hope And A Future*. Far too often, though, a family has to choose medication because they aren't aware of another way to help their precious child. Once on medication, a child is often on medication for many years as a means to control the negative symptoms they are experiencing.

The Travis family witnessed the transformation in Logan because they worked very hard to organize his central nervous system and eliminate the root cause affecting him. By removing the root cause, you reduce and often eliminate the symptoms causing so much havoc in the life of the child. The time invested into Logan's neurodevelopmental plan was worth every moment, as it gave him the rest of his life functioning optimally!

Logan was emotionally stable, academically advanced, behaviorally sound, and his processing had taken off. Logan had ZERO hyperactivity! He was a sweet, kind, courteous, and sharp young boy who was ready to fly!

**October 2012 6th/Final Evaluation Notes**
Age: 8 years 1 month
Diagnosis: ADHD – Gone!
3rd grade: Public School

Behavior and Concerns: No concerns
Cross pattern creep: Feet elevation decreased – incomplete
Primitive Reflexes (tested) not integrated: Moro

ADS . . . . . . . . . . . 6, bridged 7
ACWS . . . . . . . . . . 5
VDS . . . . . . . . . . . 7
VFD . . . . . . . . . . . 5, bridged 6

Math . . . . . . . . . . 3.6
Word Recognition . . . . 6.1
Comprehension . . . . . 5.3

Auditory Dominance . . . Left
Visual Dominance . . . . Left
Manual Dominance . . . Left
Foot Dominance . . . . . Left-Mixed

We live in a world where spending considerable amounts of money, time, and resources are spent to manage symptoms rather than resolve issues. Once in that system, the various experts tend to lock into their experiences and training. It amazed me that the occupational therapist showed no interest in pursuing the hand- change option that had so dramatically changed Logan's life. One would have thought she would be curious about how many other children might be trapped in ADHD – not because of some biochemical imbalance or family genetics, as commonly thought – but due to neurological disorganization. ADHD is considered to be a life-long condition with no cure, yet here was a boy who lost every symptom and damaging effect of ADHD, and the therapist just shrugged off the life-saving changes that had turned everything around for Logan.

Seven years later, we saw an entirely different reaction from Rebecca, who was also an occupational therapist. Rebecca witnessed an incredible turn-around her son, Aaron, made after he switched his hand dominance. Rebecca was outraged that her profession offers no training on the brain's role in dominance, a clearly essential factor in development. As we often see with a parent who has personally witnessed a transformation in a precious child, Rebecca was eager to learn more.

We first met Aaron when he was 11 years old. He had a myriad of sensory issues, including extreme touch defensiveness, couldn't stand being wet, extreme light sensitivity, and was a severe picky eater with physical tics. Aaron was usually withdrawn, keeping to himself as he had difficulty understanding social cues and assimilating into group activities, even when he knew the other children well. Having low motivation in everything he did, Aaron also tended to be negative and complaining. Rebecca's heart desire was for her son to be able to interact with others appropriately and to *"feel comfortable in his skin."* At Aaron's first evaluation, it was quite apparent he was going against his body's blueprint for dominance. When a person uses the wrong side of the brain for dominance, we often see symptoms of negativity, depression, anger, isolation, and that sense of "not being comfortable in their skin."

Four months later, Aaron had changed significantly. Mom reported that he was much more comfortable *"in his body,"* and he was eating quite well, willing to try new foods. Even bedwetting, which had plagued him occasionally, was gone. While still uncomfortable with switching dominance, Aaron was making good progress, and Rebecca reported that he was very stable and more regulated overall. She said his mood was very even keel, and he was no longer having any outbursts. Rebecca was overjoyed that Aaron had even become positive in his thinking and nature. The entire family was surprised when Aaron decided to be part of a play at school – something he would not have done previously. Aaron, who had been unable to write a story or paper for school, was now busily writing three different stories and had completed one article entirely on his own. His ability to express himself, interact with others, and participate (even enjoying) in the church's youth group was happily overwhelming for Rebecca.

A month before Aaron's next evaluation, I received a phone call from his mom. "*Who is this kid?*" were her exact words on the phone. Rebecca marveled at the changes in her son, was saying he was now laid-back, self-controlled, cooperative, easy-going, sweet, and kind. Rebecca and her husband still couldn't believe that Aaron had gone on a mission trip with their church, an opportunity that had not been remotely possible previously. They talked about his ability to express himself - even showing facial expression – had improved demonstrably. They were thrilled that Aaron could now clean his room, keep it that way, and, even more remarkable – he loved doing it! Previously, Aaron had only talked about cleaning his room, but hadn't been able to do so.

When you are disorganized internally, it is a significant challenge to be organized externally. That was all changing for Aaron with the NDApproach. I smiled when I heard the occupational therapist in Rebecca as she happily stated, "*Aaron's executive function has kicked in!*"

I was able to see the changes in person the following month at Aaron's next evaluation. The mission trip had been a great success and Aaron eagerly told me about the adventures he had experienced. Rebecca commented that his stress level was minimal, the tics he experienced had significantly reduced, and he was able to think abstractly and logically at a much higher level. Aaron was progressing wonderfully.

Aaron's family traveled extensively, so it was another eight months before I saw him again. His neurological organization was almost complete. Mom reported that nearly all of his sensory issues were gone. He had even worn a long-sleeved shirt for the first time. Rebecca loved seeing her son calm, confident, and no longer anxious. She was amazed by Aaron's ability to focus and how he thrived in his friendships. While there was still progress to make, Rebecca felt confident they could finish his journey to full neurological organization on their own.

Rebecca was delighted with the transformation in her son but understandably frustrated that as an occupational therapist, she had never received any training regarding neurological organization.

While not all transformations require changing handedness, all do require that dominance, also known as laterality, be complete. The elimination of learning challenges and disabilities require an individual to align with their correct, genetically coded, dominant side. There can be no resolution to problems experienced when a person goes "against the grain" of his or her neurological design. When this is the case, a hand change is essential. In cases where the chosen hand is the correct one and there are still substantial issues, it is often because the rest of the dominance (ear, eye, foot) has not completed correctly to match that dominant side. When laterality is incomplete, pervasive problems will abound.

## Samuel Wagner's Story
*"Negative Outlook to Positive, Happy, and Smiling!"*

Beginning in October 2015, we had an opportunity to work with a delightful 11-year-old young man who had received an ADD diagnosis three years earlier. Samuel was a kind, good-hearted, sensitive boy. He had great empathy for others but was way too hard on himself. He worried about what others thought, embarrassed easily, had a hard time sticking up for himself, and often let others push him around or make fun of him. Samuel's struggles presented as early as preschool, when teachers had shared their concerns about his social immaturity and their thoughts about his inability to handle the large class sizes of the public elementary school he would attend that fall. The school advised that Samuel should do an additional transitional year in preschool, as they were concerned that he would be overwhelmed and possibly bullied if he went to kindergarten as planned. Instead of holding him back, Collin and Marcy were able to get their son into a highly recommended charter school with only 16 children in his classroom. Unfortunately, even in this less overwhelming environment, Samuel often rolled around on the rug and made humming noises throughout that kindergarten year.

It was during third grade that Samuel received the ADD diagnosis. Marcy shared that the physician immediately offered the medication option – and he didn't even know Samuel. The doctor informed them that there were no programs or other alternatives that would help them, only medication. Samuel's parents refused the drug and the school supported them in this choice, even though Samuel would have been easier to handle on medication, and the teachers were openly frustrated with him.

School was torturous for Samuel. He had a very negative outlook on school despite being able to maintain in the accelerated fifth-grade program at the charter school. He was above grade level in reading; math was slightly below where it should be. Samuel liked math, though, despite always having to relearn long division again and again because he got "lost" in the steps and refused to show his work. His teachers described Samuel as being the most disorganized student they had ever taught.

**October 2015 1st Evaluation Notes**
Age: 11 years 3 months
Diagnosis: ADD
5th grade: Charter School – accelerated program

Behavior and Concerns: Black and white, deep thinker. Highly disorganized, emotional, sensitive. Picky eating and phobias noted.

Crawl: Incomplete
Creep: Incomplete
Primitive Reflexes (tested) not integrated: Moro

ADS . . . . . . . . . . . . 5-6
ACWS . . . . . . . . . . 4
VDS . . . . . . . . . . . 6, bridged 7
VFD . . . . . . . . . . . 5

Math . . . . . . . . . . 5.3
Word Recognition . . . . 8.7
Comprehension . . . . . 6.5

Auditory Dominance . . . Left-Mixed
Visual Dominance . . . . Right-Mixed
Manual Dominance . . . Right
Foot Dominance . . . . . Right-Mixed

Collin and Marcy were quite happy with the quick results they saw with Samuel. His ability to listen, follow directions, and increased attention span were remarkable. Marcy thought it was fabulous that Samuel was completing his work more independently and studying for tests with less help. Also daydreaming in class - which had been a real concern plaguing him for years – had significantly reduced. Samuel's memory was much stronger and his maturity had blossomed. Marcy laughed that Samuel had dropped silverware all the time but was no longer doing that. To her astonishment, he was no longer a picky eater and enjoyed an ever-expanding variety of foods in his diet. Also, I noted that his cursive writing had greatly improved, he was mumbling less, and his balance and coordination were much better.

**February 2016 2nd Evaluation Notes**
Age: 11 years 6 months
Diagnosis: ADD
5th grade: Charter School – accelerated program

Behavior and Concerns: Resistant glass-half-empty personality. Obedient. He likes alone time but now able to play with a few friends and brother. High level of maturity noted. Spelling improved.

Crawl: Serialized cross pattern – complete
Creep: Serialized cross pattern – complete
Primitive Reflexes (tested) not integrated: Moro (decreased)

ADS . . . . . . . . . . . 6-7
ACWS . . . . . . . . . . 5-6
VDS . . . . . . . . . . . 6-7
VFD . . . . . . . . . . . 7

Math . . . . . . . . . . 6.1
Word Recognition . . . . 10.9
Comprehension . . . . . 6.2

Auditory Dominance . . . Mixed
Visual Dominance . . . . Right-Mixed
Manual Dominance . . . Right
Foot Dominance . . . . . Right

Samuel's evaluation four months later showed a different picture. In that four-month period, they had only worked his program for two months, with a few activities continuing for another two weeks. During the six weeks before the evaluation, nothing from his plan had been accomplished, resulting in understandable regressions much to Collin and Marcy's dismay. Samuel was overreacting and having tantrums; he also had difficulty processing instructions from his new tennis coach. Once again, Samuel was exhibiting social disconnection and was spiraling on seemingly small matters; the mumbling that had quietly disappeared returned and was prevalent once again.

It is so difficult for parents to witness a child reverting to behaviors they thought had been conquered. However, when building new pathways and re-organizing the central nervous system, consistency is critical. Fortunately, all that was needed for Samuel to recover his progress was to actively work the program once again. Marcy said the only good thing to come out of their "falling off the program wagon" was the clear evidence about how much the ND program was helping. It was stopping their program activities that confirmed how much of a difference the NDApproach was actually making for their son.

**June 2016 3rd Evaluation Notes**
Age: 11 years 10 months
Diagnosis: ADD
5th grade: Charter School – accelerated program

Behavior and Concerns: Visibly frustrated by his negativity. Overreactions, tantrums. Social disconnect. Overly critical of peers. Less desire to interact. Spirals on seemingly small things.

Primitive Reflexes (tested) not integrated: Moro, SGR, ATNR

| | |
|---|---|
| ADS | 7 |
| ACWS | 5-6 |
| VDS | 6 |
| VFD | 6-7 |

| | |
|---|---|
| Math | 5.9 |
| Word Recognition (Level 1) | 12.9 |
| Word Recognition (Level 2) | 8.9 |
| Comprehension | 5.8 |

| | |
|---|---|
| Auditory Dominance | Mixed-Left |
| Visual Dominance | Right-Mixed |
| Manual Dominance | Right |
| Foot Dominance | Right |

Samuel's one-year-anniversary of starting ND arrived, bringing with it a much-improved young man. All the overreactions, tantrums, and emotionality had subsided substantially. He was much more stable and was also sleeping better. Collin and Marcy had been very consistent, even finally having Samuel do the dominance work seven days a week. When working to create new pathways or dominance, it is imperative to work on it every single day. Progress suffers by even one missed day. Their perseverance had landed them exceptional results for Samuel.

**October 2016 4th Evaluation Notes**
Age: 12 years 3 months
Diagnosis: ADD
6th grade: Charter School – accelerated program

Behavior and Concerns: School is going well at times, crashes other times

Primitive Reflexes (tested) not integrated: Moro, SGR
ATNR Complete

| | |
|---|---|
| ADS | 7 |
| ACWS | 6 |
| VDS | 7, bridged 8 |
| VFD | 6, bridged 7 |
| | |
| Math (Level 1) | 7.0 |
| Math (Level 2) | 6.3 |
| Word Recognition | 8.9 |
| Comprehension | 7.5 |
| | |
| Auditory Dominance | Mixed-Right |
| Visual Dominance | Right-Mixed |
| Manual Dominance | Right |
| Foot Dominance | Right |

Four months later, in February 2017, I was thrilled with what had transpired since Samuel's previous evaluation. Despite the fact that 30 to 40 percent of the plan had been accomplished this time around, Samuel showed significant changes. We've seen it often that once the dominance organization is nearing completion, things have a "domino effect," even when there is less accomplished. Samuel was happier, smiling a lot, and was so much more positive about everything! Mom happily reported a momentous improvement in the social arena. Samuel had thoroughly enjoyed his first overnight experience at a friend's house. Marcy said this was huge – he could never have done this before working an ND program. In school, Samuel was independently completing schoolwork and finally achieving good grades on tests!

Marcy shared with me for the first time a concern about an ongoing issue with Samuel. It's not unusual that as bigger problems start fading away, lesser concerns surface. Marcy explained that Samuel had always chewed on his fingers (something he didn't do during his evaluations), and she worried this nasty habit would follow him through life. I assured her Samuel was still in process, and I fully expected this issue, too, would resolve and disappear.

**February 2017 5th Evaluation Notes**
Age: 12 years 6 months
Diagnosis: ADD
6th grade: Charter School – accelerated program

Behavior and Concerns: More positive, significant social improvement, proper maturity, reading social cues. Happier!!! Smiling!!!

Primitive Reflexes (tested) not integrated: None
Moro, SGR Complete

ADS . . . . . . . . . . . 6-7
ACWS . . . . . . . . . . 5-6
VDS . . . . . . . . . . . 7, bridged 8
VFD . . . . . . . . . . . 6, bridged 7

Math – not tested
Word Recognition . . . . 9.9
Comprehension . . . . . 8.8

Auditory Dominance . . . Mixed-Right
Visual Dominance . . . . Right-Mixed
Manual Dominance . . . Right
Foot Dominance . . . . . Right

Sometimes "life" invades itself and time gets away from us. That happened with the Wagner family. It was nearly a year before I saw them again. Even though they hadn't come in for so long, they had been faithful in completing the plan last designed for Samuel. I was amazed at their perseverance in sticking with the same activities for so long without "burning out."

Marcy was effusive about all the improvements Samuel was experiencing. There were incredibly exciting changes to share indeed! So much so, I chose to highlight these results as "bullets" of hope for others – they are listed on the next page. There is hope that the challenges your child (or yourself) is living with can be significantly reduced and often even eliminated.

- Confidence increased!
- Stress, anxiety decreased!
- More relaxed, in control of his emotions!
- Foggy days "few and far between"!
- Great attitude!
- Willing to try new experiences!

- No longer depressed or anxious regarding school and homework!
- Most days good because he is taking in information and understanding it!
- His attention span for learning and retention of the information improved!
- All schoolwork independently accomplished and done well!
- His teacher used a paragraph he wrote as an example for the entire seventh-grade class!
- He is articulating and expressing himself very well!
- He is no longer shunned by classmates when paired up with them!
- Mature for his age!
- He is no longer biting his fingers!

**January 2018 6th Evaluation Notes**
Age: 13 years 6 months
Diagnosis: ADD
6th grade: Charter School – accelerated program

Behavior and Concerns: Bullets highlighted above

| | |
|---|---|
| ADS | 7, bridged 8 |
| ACWS | 5-6 |
| VDS | 7, bridged 8 |
| VFD | 7, bridged 8 |
| Math – not tested | |
| Word Recognition | 11.3 |
| Comprehension | 10.4 |
| Auditory Dominance | Right |
| Visual Dominance | Right |
| Manual Dominance | Right |
| Foot Dominance | Left-Mixed |

The Wagner family continued to be faithful to the NDApproach plan for Samuel. It is essential, for successful re-organization, to monitor and change the plan on a timely basis, as the brain does well with fresh input. After nearly a year of being on the same set of activities, and potentially spending time and effort on activities no longer needed, they were all ready for something new and different. Marcy and Collin also knew they were coming to the homestretch with their son, and this was no time to lighten up.

When I saw Samuel next, he was exactly two months shy of turning 14. He was having some sugar cravings, which was new, and some issues with acne. The primitive Moro reflex had resurfaced, which can occasionally happen, especially with Samuel at the age of considerable growth and physical changes for boys. Because one of the many symptoms of a retained Moro reflex is sugar cravings, I decided to recheck the integration of it.

Our meeting in May 2018 was an exciting evaluation because Samuel tested completely right-side dominant. For the first time in his life, his neurological organization had lined up. His ear, eye, and foot were solidly right dominant, matching the genetic coded right hand. Samuel's reading word recognition and comprehension had soared three to four grade levels. When parents are concerned with their child's failing grades, I try to reassure them not to worry. When dominance comes in, the academics follow. It isn't that Samuel suddenly learned three to four grades of reading and comprehension, but that he was now able to access, retrieve, and utilize the information previously acquired. It had been "lost" in the inefficient storage system of his brain. At this evaluation, Samuel was ready to tackle once again the math test, and he did it on the harder, Level 2 worksheet. At the end of the meeting, Marcy happily confided what an absolute pleasure it was to be with her son.

**May 2018 7th Evaluation Notes**
Age: 13 years 10 months
Diagnosis: ADD
6th grade: Charter School – accelerated program

Behavior and Concerns: Confidence continues to increase. Extremely polite. Extremely logical thinker.

Primitive Reflexes (tested) not integrated: Moro

ADS . . . . . . . . . . . . 7, bridged 8
ACWS . . . . . . . . . . 6
VDS . . . . . . . . . . . 7-8
VFD . . . . . . . . . . . 7

Math (timed) . . . . . . 7.4
Math (untimed) . . . . . 10.1
Word Recognition . . . . 13.2
Comprehension . . . . . 12.3

Auditory Dominance . . . Right
Visual Dominance . . . . Right
Manual Dominance . . . Right
Foot Dominance . . . . . Right

September 2018 was Samuel's exit evaluation. He was 14 and had taken off. His right-side dominance had locked in, the Moro reflex had reintegrated, and his academics were solid. Samuel developed a great sense of humor and his teachers adored him; what a change from the days when teachers were so frustrated with him. What a great transformation for Samuel! The results of his hard work and diligence were apparent in his ability to now go through life with great ease.

**September 2018 8th/FinalEvaluation Notes**
Age: 14 years 2 months
Diagnosis: ADD – Gone!
7th grade: Charter School – accelerated program

Behavior and Concerns: Maturity great!

Primitive Reflexes (tested) not integrated: None
Moro Complete

ADS . . . . . . . . . . . 7
ACWS . . . . . . . . . . 6
VDS . . . . . . . . . . . 7-8
VFD . . . . . . . . . . . 8, bridged 9

Math (timed) . . . . . . 7.1
Math (untimed) – not tested
Word Recognition . . . . 13.8
Comprehension . . . . . 12.8

Auditory Dominance . . . Right
Visual Dominance . . . . Right
Manual Dominance . . . Right
Foot Dominance . . . . . Right

Watching children and adults struggle from the symptoms of ADD and ADHD is heartbreaking. It's even more tragic knowing that millions are suffering from these no-hope labels and who never hear about the life-changing impact of achieving neurological organization. Struggles with ADD and ADHD can fade away and disappear. Negative attitudes can turn around and become positive because there is more than just personality in play here. Social awareness and appropriateness are achievable for those who lack these essential skills. Hyperactivity, as well as attention and focus issues can, and do go away. Those who are failing in school can have hopes of attending college and seeing their dreams materialize. While drugs may offer a temporary resolution, they do not need to be – and never should be – the only answer.

Medication only masks and covers up the symptoms – symptoms which can be eliminated through properly stimulating and organizing the brain.

It would be interesting, although impossible, to do double-blind studies, but there is no way to take a person and see an outcome with and without neurodevelopmental intervention. What we can chart, though, are the results of those persons who correctly align their dominance, increase their processing, eliminate sensory dysfunction, and fully organize their central nervous system compared with those who do not follow the path of central nervous system reorganization. Unfortunately, we have children and adults who have come to *Hope And A Future* for neurodevelopmental programs but do not see it through to completion. It always breaks our hearts to hear about such a person years later who is still struggling and sometimes even failing tragically in life. More often, though, we receive heartwarming testimonies from people who graduated their NDAppoach program years earlier and are now thriving. We treasure these updates and will now close this chapter with two timely, "years later" updates we just received.

> *"We are so grateful for the successes that your approach helped to facilitate for our son Christopher. He came to Hope And A Future when he was 4 with ADHD, dyslexia, dysgraphia, sensory processing issues, and gross and fine motor issues. We worked your program for several years.*
>
> *Last year, Christopher was named by his high school faculty as one of the two top graduates in his senior class based on academics and character. He is currently a pre-med student and hopes to become an osteopathic doctor.*
>
> *People who did not know him when he was a little boy cannot believe that he could possibly have come into the world with all of those challenges."*

## Ryan and Kyle's Journey
*"Hope, Success, and Incredible Futures"*

I first met Linda Kane and learned about the NeuroDevelopmental Approach in 2009 at MassHOPE, Massachusetts annual homeschool convention. Linda's company name, *Hope And A Future* is undoubtedly appropriate – they had been the first one to give us hope rather than just more labels!

My son, Ryan, had been labeled ADD Inattentive Type. He had no hyperactivity, social, or impulse issues. Thankfully, Ryan was very laid back, easy-going, funny, and a great kid to be around. He was 15, in the 9th grade, and we had been homeschooling since 6th grade (our fourth year). We noticed that Ryan was very, very bright at a young age, and when tested at the end of 3rd grade, they said he was "beyond his years" in some of the answers he gave.

However, learning was very hard for Ryan. Although he had a strong auditory system in 3rd grade at age 9, he couldn't retain anything he read. He had been very good with phonics and read quite well – just nothing "stuck." On his own, he would read science or history fact books with pictures and little "blurbs," which he did great with – he was a walking random fact expert! He hated chapter books as he got bored halfway through, would put them down, and would never finish them. He was, without a doubt, the child whose "file cabinet" would spill out all over the floor. The filing was random, and retrieval was frustrating. (Editor Note: the file cabinet reference is referring to an analogy used by Linda in her talk comparing it to a neurologically disorganized person)

I remember telling Linda that my son, Ryan was a poster child for her presentation's slide that stated:
"I know My Child is Intelligent but ...."
    Why is she so disorganized?
    Why is his room such a mess?
    Why does she lose everything?
    Why is his schoolwork in chaos?
    Why does she know something one day and not the next?
    Why is everything so hard for her/him?

Even though he had lost some of his auditory ability over time, Ryan was able to read and retain more on his own. Math, on the other hand, was a nightmare. He had completed a standardized test, and when I went through the math section, I found 31 problems he had gotten wrong. I remember my tears that flowed that day like they happened yesterday. I knew that he knew the computation of all he had gotten wrong. He had learned it! I ended up writing all the incorrect problems on a plain piece of paper and gave it to him a few days later. Ryan got over 90% of those 31 problems correct without hesitation. He was having a good day that day. *Most* of his days were bad days, though. He would say, "*I can't concentrate,*" and he couldn't. He wanted to, he tried so hard, and Ryan absolutely looked like he was concentrating, but the information was going nowhere.

I was exhausted, hit high levels of frustration, and could only imagine how much worse it was for Ryan. At one point that year, he just had given up on school. It was depressing for me to teach, knowing all the information I taught went into that "big room" where the files were dumped out and scattered everywhere, and may never be retrieved again. It was even more frustrating for him. The school tested Ryan at the end of 3rd grade, and they told me, *"He files things away but has no way to retrieve that information in an organized manner."*

We learned about neurodevelopment at the end of Ryan's 9th grade year. I also had an 8th grade daughter and 6th grade son and giving them what they needed was always extremely challenging for me as Ryan ate up all of my time. I literally needed to sit with him and encourage him to keep him focused, or a simple task still wouldn't be done two hours later. It just didn't get done. He couldn't even take in any direction I would give him, even if repeated multiple times, and I patiently used only a few, gently spoken words. Teaching him was like riding a bike that doesn't coast. Unless I was next to him "peddling" (keeping him on task and focused), he would go nowhere. Even when I was right there, it was slow and challenging. Algebra was often an hour-long class of complete one-on-one, with us only getting through two problems – and Ryan did not even do those independently. One typical class day always took us a week. Independently done work, apart from me, never happened – ever!

Having reached exhaustion and desperation, I was willing to do whatever it took to help Ryan. Below is a portion of the first email I had sent to *Hope And A Future* after hearing Linda at MassHope.

> *I bought your DVD's, went through them twice, and took 30 pages of notes. I read through much of your information on your website (possibly the whole thing). Is there anything else you suggest I should be doing or reading? School was extremely hard for me, too – I'm probably a lot like what you shared about yourself – a good student, but working way too hard. I'll do whatever it takes to move Ryan forward to learning and functioning normally. I could relate to what you said about "coping and compensation." And what we currently are living through definitely has me feeling like I can't cope and compensate much more.*
>
> *I have put together a program for Ryan based on what I have learned from you. However, if you think I should bring him in for an evaluation – I'm willing to do that, too. I don't want to waste any more of his time. Ryan has*

*three more years of high school left, but honestly, I've had to let go of the expectation he'll graduate on time just so I can sleep at night without the pressure of having to do what seems impossible for us right now – getting through high school on time. Honestly, I have days I wonder how he'll get through high school at all. That is really sad because I know there is a very, very bright child in there – I just have not been too successful at tapping into what I know is there.*

*I'm so appreciative of all you do – I'm spreading your information to everyone I know who I think will benefit. I would love to have all the special education people see what you do!!*

*Thank you so much,*
*Caroline*

Ryan is now 26 years old and we know the rest of his ND story. We had decided our best course of action was to have Ryan evaluated through *Hope And A Future*, and he finished his neurodevelopment program in just 20 months. Upon completion, Ryan then went to a neurodevelopmental optometrist, Dr. Mann, that Linda had recommended. He needed prism glasses. With the prism glasses and several months of reading therapy, Ryan could read at an early college speed. Ryan finished his GED in the spring of 2012 and finished high school "on time!"

Ryan then completed a strenuous program called LIFT, Leaders in Further Training, during the 2012/2013 school year. They studied the Bible, Theology, and Applied Missions. They did many outdoor adventures, climbing several of the high peaks in the Adirondack mountains, climbing, hiking, and completing two mission trips to the Dominican Republic and Ecuador.

Upon returning home from his "gap year," Ryan began his career as a plumber. He applied to the plumber's union in Boston, which gets about 300 applicants for the 30 available positions. Ryan was chosen, completed a five-year apprenticeship, became a licensed plumber (passing the difficult licensing exam on the first try), and bought a home all in the spring of 2019 at the age of 25. Ryan told me he's the "human calculator" while working and laying out a job. He can add mixed fractions in his head. All this from the kid who could never answer 3x4 in high school! He is currently working in Boston, loves his career choice, and is doing wonderfully in life. Ryan is very involved in his church and enjoys the outdoor adventures of hiking, kayaking, and running.

Although Ryan's story is the most dramatic, we also put his younger brother through the ND program. He saw the difference in his brother and begged to do the same. Kyle's issues were very different. He struggled much less in school but had sensory issues that made life difficult. We've eliminated them and made his world a much better experience. He can focus better, which was a challenge even though not nearly as bad as his older brother. Kyle also needed prism glasses, as he didn't see things in front of him appropriately in space. He now retains what he reads much better. Kyle finished his ND program in 12 months and is very grateful. He is currently studying to be a neurodevelopmentalist with Little Giant Steps and plans to start schools for special needs kids in third world countries. He also did the LIFT program like his older brother, and during his mission trip to the Dominican Republic, he spent his time in what they believe is the only special needs school in the entire country. Ironically, they were doing neurodevelopment with the children, and Kyle was probably the only "LIFTer" who would have recognized what they were doing. He was the only one of the 30 in his group placed at that school – all the others served in different capacities at different locations. The school was the size of a house, and they work with only a handful of children. All the other special needs kids in the Dominican Republic are sadly locked in a room all day while their impoverished parents work. Kyle plans to plant multiple special needs schools where they are so desperately needed, and he plans to train workers to apply the neurodevelopmental techniques.

It's incredible to think of all God may do through Ryan's struggle to literally change the course of who knows how many lives. The story continues as my boys walk their successful journeys.

CHAPTER SIX

# Eradicating Learning Disabilities and Challenges

*All things are possible to him that believeth.*
Mark 9:23 – King James Version

Learning issues abound today. When children experience difficulties that cannot be explained, they often receive a label. A label provides an easy reason, or more accurately, an easy excuse for those unexplained issues. Labels are symptomatic identifications that lower expectations. In turn, those lower expectations can significantly limit an individual's achievement. Every year, as I am reading history forms for new clients, I invariably see a diagnosis that I have never heard of before. It seems that a great effort is underway to identify and categorize symptoms and struggles rather than eradicate them. The weight of these labels have the potential of crippling those who carry them. The number of children who are afflicted by these detrimental labels is staggering.

**Learning disabilities** do not discriminate; they impact **children** of all ethnicities and income levels. They *can* run in families. They are not generally treatable via medicine…***You do not grow out of a learning disability***. Nov 30, 2017 Medicinenet.com

Statements like the one above from MedicineNet are commonplace and they leave our children without hope. While it appears that learning problems may run in families, when we have worked with entire families, we have seen the learning issues go away, whether it appears inherited or not. It is true you do not grow out of a learning disability – you work your way out of it by appropriately stimulating and organizing the brain. Unfortunately, millions of children are needlessly floundering, struggling, and often failing due to lack of understanding the fundamental basics of neurological organization.

*In 2017–18, the number of students ages 3-21 who received special education services under the Individuals with Disabilities Education Act (IDEA) was 7.0 million, or 14 percent of all public school students. Among students*

*receiving special education services, 34 percent had specific learning disabilities. (Updated May 2019)*
**National Center for Educational Statistics (NCES) nces.ed.gov**

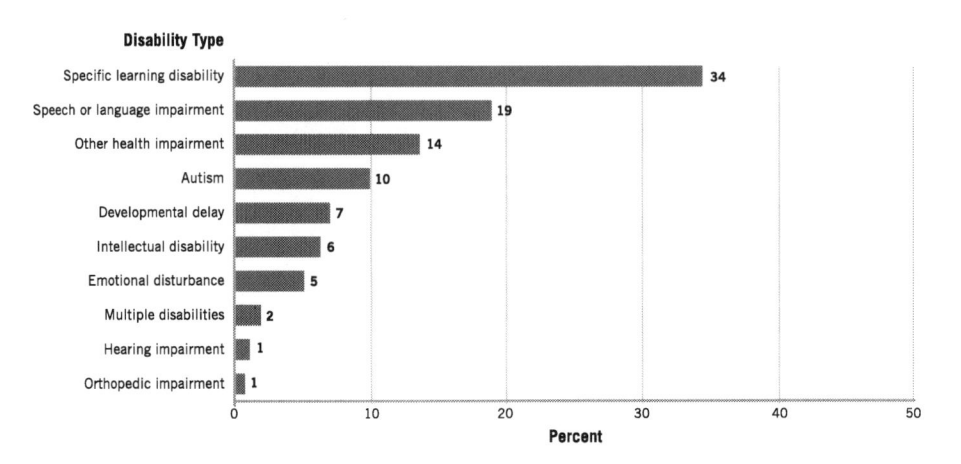

**Disability Type**

| Disability | Percent |
|---|---|
| Specific learning disability | 34 |
| Speech or language impairment | 19 |
| Other health impairment | 14 |
| Autism | 10 |
| Developmental delay | 7 |
| Intellectual disability | 6 |
| Emotional disturbance | 5 |
| Multiple disabilities | 2 |
| Hearing impairment | 1 |
| Orthopedic impairment | 1 |

Percent

Many of the families who come to us, arrive with officially diagnosed labels. Considerably more come experiencing unidentified learning challenges. The government generates its statistics based on public school enrollments, without considering those who are home-educated or in private schools. That can only mean the numbers are vastly understated. As appalling as that is, the simple truth is that there are a whole lot of children struggling, and the current system is inadequate at helping them.

We worked with a family for several years who had five of their seven children experiencing learning issues and additionally, who had aligned incorrectly to their brain's blueprint for dominance. They had started their NDApproach adventure by bringing their two daughters to be evaluated. Once the girls had successfully changed their hands and had nearly completed their neurological reorganization, the family brought in two of their sons and continued bringing in the boys until I had evaluated all seven children.

This family was part of a university-model school and had asked me to speak with parents from that school who had expressed an interest in what the family was doing. It was an intriguing time as eight families jumped into ND together and eagerly committed to doing NDApproach programs with their children. They were relieved to have found a way to help their children get past the issues hindering them, and they were delighted to have a built-in support system. All of these children had struggled for years, and time seemed to be running out as they were high-school age. I found it fascinating that seven of the eight children needed hand dominance changes. Thankfully, all eight went on to successful graduation from ND, and their lives were no longer burdened by the limitations they had suffered with for so long. After completing their programs, their futures were wide open!

The following year, I received a phone call from Teresa, a mother whose daughter attended the same university-model school. She explained that she had seen the remarkable changes in the children who had gone through *Hope And A Future's* program and eagerly wanted to do an ND program with her daughter. Teresa felt fortunate to have learned of this approach while her daughter was still only in fifth grade. However, Teresa informed me, she was not the least bit interested in changing her daughter's handedness. Now, I do understand how radical a hand change appears to someone who has not had decades witnessing the transformations I have been privileged to observe. I secretly hoped Faith was correct in her right-side dominance choice, and I let out a sigh of relief at her first evaluation when it appeared that she was appropriately right-handed. Despite the struggles, Faith was above her grade level academically and tested in the top 98 percent on standardized testing. It had been tough for her to get there and then required even greater efforts to stay there.

## Faith Connor's Story
*"Timid and Shy to Confident and Capable"*

Faith's initial program was designed to organize the central nervous system's lower levels, reinforce right-side dominance, and work on her processing abilities.

### July 2013 1st Evaluation Notes
Age: 11 years 11 months
Diagnosis: No formal diagnosis Dyslexia suspected
5th grade complete: Homeschool University Model

Concerns and Behavior: 1st concerns were at eight years old reading difficulties. Won't look at people when she speaks to them, especially adults. Occasionally bossy with peers. Sweet and kind.

Crawl: Homolateral
Creep: Incomplete
Primitive Reflexes (tested) not integrated: Moro, SGR

ADS . . . . . . . . . . . 6
ACWS . . . . . . . . . . 5
VDS . . . . . . . . . . . 6
VFD . . . . . . . . . . . 6

Math (timed) . . . . . . 6.3
Math (untimed) . . . . . 6.8
Word Recognition . . . . 8.5
Comprehension . . . . . 8.1

Auditory Dominance . . . Mixed
Visual Dominance . . . . Mixed
Manual Dominance . . . Right
Foot Dominance . . . . . Right-Mixed

Faith's second evaluation really surprised us. While initially everything had reinforced right-side dominance, her body had started organizing to the left side after doing the lower-level program activities. Apparently, Faith's genetic blueprint had never emerged and after only four months of ND stimulation, the design had surfaced, showing her to be left-side dominant. Stunned, Teresa took the revelation regarding dominance well. She had seen enough improvement in her daughter already, that she was willing to trust the process, but this was a lot for her to take in. In the end, we decided the best course was to give Faith's central nervous system another four months of stimulation, which included providing her with opportunities to practice using her left hand while not entirely switching her dominance. Faith would daily practice writing, drawing, coloring, and eating with her left hand for short periods. I was confident the brain would clearly show the dominance coding by her next evaluation.

### November 2013 2nd Evaluation Notes
Age: 12 years 3 months
Diagnosis: No formal diagnosis Dyslexia suspected
6th grade: Homeschool University Model

Concerns and Behavior: Overall displaying a positive attitude. Socially young. Poor eye contact, especially when greeting people. Stutter with reading and slow speed of reading. Spelling is atrocious. Concerned will not be able to keep up next year in a school setting.

Crawl: Homolateral, homologous and cross patterns alternated
Creep: Incomplete

Primitive Reflexes (tested) not integrated: Moro
Spinal Galant complete

| | |
|---|---|
| ADS | 6, bridged 7 |
| ACWS | 5, bridged 6 |
| VDS | 6-7 |
| VFD | 6 |
| | |
| Math (timed) | 6.1 |
| Math (untimed) | 8.5 |
| Word Recognition | 9.9 |
| Comprehension | 8.8 |
| | |
| Auditory Dominance | Mixed-Left |
| Visual Dominance | Left-Mixed |
| Manual Dominance | Right |
| Foot Dominance | Right |

By Faith's third evaluation, Teresa started to second guess what they were doing. She saw some positive changes academically and socially, but it seemed like so much work. And, much to her frustration, Faith's spelling was not showing any progress. However, the results of that evaluation surprised Teresa, and she was once again highly motivated to keep going by the end of our discussion because Faith's math score had jumped three grade levels, and her reading comprehension and word recognition had bounced up two levels. Faith's CNS was unquestionably organizing to the left side, so the plan would be to go full force in that direction. Remarkably, Faith's auditory dominance had switched entirely to the left, with her visual dominance nearly left-side complete. That happened without even doing any occluding to help the pathways build and encourage changing sides. Even Faith was surprised at how comfortable using her left hand had become. It was time to begin entirely switching over to left-side dominance, and both Teresa and Faith were in total agreement with that decision.

### March 2014 3rd Evaluation Notes
Age: 12 years 7 months
Diagnosis: No formal diagnosis Dyslexia suspected
6th grade: Homeschool University Model

Concerns and Behavior: 2nd guessing if they should continue with ND. Reading with hesitation. Spelling

Crawl: Significant improvement
Creep: Near complete
Primitive Reflexes (tested) not integrated: Moro (initial integration)

ADS . . . . . . . . . . . 7, bridged 8
ACWS . . . . . . . . . . 5, bridged 6
VDS . . . . . . . . . . . 6-7
VFD . . . . . . . . . . . 5, bridged 6

Math (timed) . . . . . . 6.9
Math (untimed) . . . . . 11.3
Word Recognition . . . . 11.3
Comprehension . . . . . 10.2

Auditory Dominance . . . Left
Visual Dominance . . . . Left-Mixed
Manual Dominance . . . Left-Mixed
Foot Dominance . . . . . Mixed-Left

I was eager to see Faith again, curious as to how the left-side transition was going. I hadn't heard from the Connor family since the last evaluation, so I had no idea what to expect when they arrived four months later. I was relieved to hear that they were continuing the course to left-side dominance. Teresa expressed some concern that the switch was not making faster progress and she worried about Faith's slow reading pace and lack of math comprehension. In addition, her frustration over Faith's poor spelling was quite evident. "*Will she EVER be able to spell?*" was her desperate question.

Often, a person making a dominance switch, does not exhibit all the changes hoped for until the transition is complete. I assured Teresa that Faith was changing over at a breakneck pace, and that all the symptoms of Faith's disorganization would disappear when her laterality completed. I encouraged them to keep going; everything was proceeding very nicely.

### July 2014 4th Evaluation Notes
Age: 12 years 11 months
Diagnosis: No formal diagnosis Dyslexia suspected
6th grade complete: Homeschool University Model

Concerns and Behavior: Dominance change progress. The slowness of reading and lack of math comprehension. Spelling

Crawl: Serialized cross pattern – complete
Creep: Near complete
Primitive Reflexes (tested) not integrated: Moro (near-complete integration)

ADS . . . . . . . . . . . . 7
ACWS . . . . . . . . . . 5, bridged 6
VDS . . . . . . . . . . . 6-7
VFD . . . . . . . . . . . 6

Math (timed) . . . . . . 7.4
Math (untimed) . . . . . 11.8
Word Recognition . . . . 11.3
Comprehension . . . . . 11.8

Auditory Dominance . . . Left
Visual Dominance . . . . Left-Mixed
Manual Dominance . . . Left-Mixed
Foot Dominance . . . . . Mixed-Left

At Faith's fifth evaluation, spelling still topped Teresa's list of concerns because there had been no improvement whatsoever. Teresa had a hard time believing that the spelling would ever improve, and it was difficult for me to convince her to hang on until the end. On another front, though, Faith noted that she felt more confident when talking with people; Teresa added that Faith's eye contact with adults had significantly improved. We all celebrated that day, despite some eye-dominance regression, because Faith's left ear and left hand had fully become dominant. "Now," I told them, "get ready for the 'domino effect.'" With her left hand wholly dominant, changes were going to come quickly.

### November 2014 5th Evaluation Notes
Age: 13 years 3 months
Diagnosis: No formal diagnosis Dyslexia suspected
7th grade: Homeschool University Model

Concerns and Behavior: The progress of switching dominance left, slow reading speed and math comprehension, stagnation with visual processing. SPELLING!

Creep: Serialized cross pattern – complete
Primitive Reflexes (tested) not integrated: Moro (near-complete integration)

ADS . . . . . . . . . . . . 7, bridged 8
ACWS . . . . . . . . . . 5-6
VDS . . . . . . . . . . . 6, bridged 7
VFD . . . . . . . . . . . 6, bridged 7

Math (timed) . . . . . . 6.7
Math (untimed) . . . . . 13.8

Word Recognition . . . . 10.5
Comprehension . . . . . 12.8 (maximum score achievable)

Auditory Dominance . . . Left
Visual Dominance . . . . Left-Mixed
Manual Dominance . . . Left
Foot Dominance . . . . . Left-Mixed

It never ceases to amaze me, watching all the issues and concerns disappear once laterality with the design of the body is complete. I knew Faith had fully achieved dominance when I saw her walk in. She had a new poise about her. Faith now had great posture, held her head up, and looked directly into my eyes when we talked. She was calm, relaxed, and confident! Teresa said, "*Oh, and the spelling clicked in two weeks ago.*" She laughed as she described her joy when out of nowhere, her daughter finally could spell and spell well! Teresa was thrilled with Faith's maturity – she was now a capable, bright young woman no longer plagued with learning obstacles.

### March 2015 6th/Final Evaluation Notes
Age: 13 years 7 months
Diagnosis: No formal diagnosis Dyslexia suspected – Gone!
7th grade: Homeschool University Model

Concerns and Behavior: Confident and Capable! Spelling had "clicked" two weeks earlier and was no longer a concern. No hesitation, stammer, or slowness with reading. Math comprehension doing well.

Primitive Reflexes (tested) not integrated: Moro (slight)

ADS . . . . . . . . . . . 7, bridged 8
ACWS . . . . . . . . . . 5-6
VDS . . . . . . . . . . . 7, bridged 8
VFD . . . . . . . . . . . 6

Math (timed) . . . . . . 7.4
Math (untimed) . . . . . 13.8
Word Recognition . . . . 11.6

Auditory Dominance . . . Left
Visual Dominance . . . . Left
Manual Dominance . . . Left
Foot Dominance . . . . . Left

As I have already disclosed, I have an intense loathing of testing, even though we do use it in a minimal measure. Nonetheless, our current culture relies too much on excessive testing and its often- erroneous results. Testing is not an accurate measure of an individual's knowledge, understanding, or intelligence, especially for someone experiencing neurological inefficiency that results in learning challenges. We should not be a one-fit "cookie-cutter" society! The belief that there is one mold for all is absurd, as everyone is a uniquely created individual. We all have different strengths, callings, and gifts. The notion that we should all excel in every area is ridiculous. Yet, these are the common expectations. Rather than focus on what a student does well, our system tends to put all the emphasis on what they don't do well, often seeming to punish a child with loss of recess time or by requiring an after school stay to work more on what is under par. When someone is doing something poorly, doing more of it does not help and tends to result in frustration rather than benefiting the situation. It's like expecting water from an empty well; it just can't work.

I have had the privilege of working with more involved children for decades. These precious, wonderful children usually come with genetic conditions, autism, or brain injury, and are whom we lovingly call "marathoners." Other children might be long term because I provide their homeschool oversight. There are also times when the desired results don't manifest quickly due to other contributing non-developmental factors such as health concerns, allergies, leaky-gut syndrome, biochemical imbalances, and metabolism disrupters, to name a few. Under these circumstances, some of our learning-challenged children have become marathoners, as well.

Phillip was a "marathoner" due to a combination of developmental and non-developmental reasons. We first began working with Phillip in 1999, when he was seven years old. He was a highly emotional, frustrated, and discouraged young boy. While math seemed to come relatively easy for him, he was not learning to read. He often confused the letters, reversed them, or forgot their names and sounds completely. The family was attempting to teach Phillip to read phonetically, which was an impossible way for him to learn because of his significantly low processing ability. Phillip had mixed dominance, in addition to immature processing, and the family described him as *just barely above water."* On top of that, Phillip was coping with severe allergies and asthma.

It was painful to hear Phillip attempting to sound out words from one evaluation to another. His first recorded word recognition score was 1.3, and his score remained at the first-grade level for two more years. Math, which initially seemed to be easy, had stalled, barely showing a nominal change. During those two years of our working together, Phillip's auditory processing was stagnant and his visual processing was only minimally better. What first appeared to be an easy organization to the left for dominance – as Phillip was far more left than right-sided – had been met with the central nervous system's full resistance to change. Then, at Phillip's second anniversary doing an ND program, his ear and eye dominance substantially shifted to the right side. Phillip's family was hesitant to switch paths with dominance, hoping the dominance sliding to the right was just a fluke. Four months later, his reading level had finally crossed the second-grade barrier, and his math had increased by a year and a half. Phillip's parents took this as evidence to stay the course encouraging left-side dominance.

However, four months later, there was no ignoring the brain's signals to right-side dominance. Phillip's visual dominance had dramatically switched right; his auditory dominance had changed to be more right than left, and he had occasionally begun using his right foot for dominance. The brain is quite amazing!  For nearly three years, we had attempted to organize Phillip's laterality to the left side. Pushing to the wrong side had caused the brain to work overtime in getting its system to align correctly and establish to the right. With the changes happening, we recorded more than a year increase in word recognition, taking only four months to push into a third grade reading level. The improvements we saw were not just in academics. Phillip's behavior and attitude also had significantly improved. His negative moods and depression were at an all-time low.

Right-side laterality didn't completely lock in for Phillip during the next few years, most likely due to the physiological concerns he had. While asthma and allergies had reduced, they still affected him. There was good news for Phillip, though. He was able to access the benefits of the neurological organization without having achieved it 100 percent. By 14, Phillip was reading and comprehending at the eighth-grade level! Reading had not come easily, but he was now enjoying it. Overreactions, frustration, and bad attitudes were a thing of the past. He was a mature, caring, and responsible young man. He was able to self-regulate quickly the few times the need arose. His mother confided to me, even though she always loved her son, he had been quite exasperating and challenging to be around. She now spoke of how wonderful a young man he was, and that spending time with him was an absolute delight!

It had taken many years for Phillip to achieve neurological organization, which is highly unusual. Physiological conditions, compounding the incorrect blueprint for a few years, had all factored into the extended timeframe. However, it was well worth all of their efforts as Phillip successfully went on to college, married a wonderful woman, and is the proud father of three precious girls. You can bet Phillip and his wife will make sure their little ones go through all the appropriate developmental stages correctly!

Scott and Grace were entirely different stories when it came to the time it took to get through their NDApproach programs. They were both determined, committed, and ready to leave their struggles behind. Just the hope of not doing everything so painfully and exasperatingly slow was more than enough motivation for both of them.

When I first met Scott, he was highly competitive. As part of a swim team, Scott was well trained and conditioned. He liked to be the leader and wanted to make the rules. He vehemently hated losing and was unwilling to share with anyone. I have to laugh as I remember back to his first evaluation in May 2019, when he was 12 years old. As part of the assessment of foot dominance, I ask the children to "gently kick" a ball to me – Scott almost took my head off with his kick! It had been a close call for sure.

One piece of information on his history form jumped out and had grabbed my attention. His mom, Susan, noted that handwriting was a chore and Scott detested it. She stated he wrote like a first-grader, big and messy, and he had an "iron fist grasp" on the pencil. Nothing she did could convince him to hold the pencil correctly, and to be honest, nothing she would say could ever change that because it took that intensity level for his brain to realize that he was holding a pencil. This discovery had been a big flag for me regarding Scott's handedness.

Susan also disclosed that they suspected dyslexia, which ran in the family, but they had never gone through any formal testing. Despite slowly working his way through a reading program specifically designed for persons with dyslexia and spelling issues and having completed vision therapy, Scott was still struggling, highly stressed, and experiencing irrational fears.

He also was a rather picky eater; his mother had further described. Foods had to have a precise texture and taste, or he wouldn't eat them. Since Susan did most of their cooking from scratch, it was easy for sauces to be different consistencies and baked, toasted, or grilled foods to have differing levels of color and crispness – all things that could bother him enough to deter his eating. Of particular interest to me was the fact that he had not become picky with food until he was nearly seven. Seven is often the age when the genetic coding for dominance surfaces, and if that coding were opposite to what the child had chosen, symptoms and problems would begin from that point forward.

My suspicions regarding Scott's handedness appeared to be well-founded. While he did all trained manual function right-handed, he naturally used his left hand for many unskilled tasks. The same was true for his foot dominance. While his expeditious kick was right-footed, he hopped, stood, and lead all with his left foot. Additionally, other, subtle tell-tale signs indicated that Scott was supposed to be left-dominant, so there was no question regarding that his first INP would focus on switching to left-side dominance.

There was fantastic news during his second evaluation – Scott had switched his hand entirely left in under four months! Susan relayed that he never even needed reminders for using his left hand for writing, eating, brushing his teeth, etc. He was writing with a much better pencil grasp, good fine-motor movement, and was no longer complaining about his arm hurting, as it had done in the initial stage of dominant use. The letter reversals that had always plagued him were going away. Even his excessive competitiveness had decreased to more appropriate levels. Although, it seems there was some advantage to his being competitive, as he currently holds the record for the fastest hand change I have ever witnessed!

## Grace's Story
*"No longer feeling overwhelmed!"*

Grace's mom, Jenny, was already a pro at ND, having taken her son successfully through to completion with his *Hope And A Future* program. Jenny was quite excited to be able to embark on this journey with Grace, who concerned her greatly.

At sixteen and a half, Grace was accomplished in school, dually attending home school and a community college. She sang in the choir at church and played the piano, as well as the violin splendidly. As Jenny worked with her son, it occurred to her that Grace needed ND, too. Grace was doing well academically; it just took excruciatingly long to learn, often using most waking hours of each day. She would need to read, re-read, and re-read everything again, multiple times, to gain understanding and "make it stick." She did just about everything at a snail's pace, always trying to have it perfect. Her mom wrote, "*If perfection can't be accomplished, she just gives up and doesn't do anything.*" Jenny also informed me that Grace procrastinated, was easily distracted – and a "*dreamer,*" she said. Grace wasted considerable amounts of time with non-priority issues apparently unable to discern the essential tasks. Grace rarely carried out her plans or schedule. And, her mother sighed, "*She overthinks everything!*"

At Grace's first evaluation, we discovered the culprit for all her difficulties. She was severely mixed-dominant. It was no wonder Grace was struggling so much with information recall. Everything she was learning was going in for storage through her left eye and ear, depositing in the opposite side of the brain. The right hand ultimately connected with the hemisphere of the brain that did not contain one shred of the information learned. In such a case, when wanting to use the information stored, such as during a test, the brain has to go searching to find that incorrectly stored information. Once found, the retrieved data then has to cross the corpus callosum and be placed in the correct hemisphere connected with the hand so it can be accessed. The entire process takes a long time and is exhausting!

**March 2018 1st Evaluation Notes**
Age: 16 years 6 months
Diagnosis: None
Dual Enrollment: High School and Community College

Concerns and Behavior: Kind, compassionate, and helpful. Great self-control and loving. Responsible, patient, and very direct. Extremely slow, taking more than twice as long as should be with schoolwork and chores. Perfectionistic, procrastinator, and highly disorganized with personal things. Enormous stress levels.

Crawl: Incomplete
Creep: Incomplete
Primitive Reflexes (tested) not integrated: Babinski, Moro, STNR, Amphibian

```
ADS . . . . . . . . . . . 6-7
ACWS . . . . . . . . . . 5-6
VDS . . . . . . . . . . . 6
VFD . . . . . . . . . . . 5
```

```
Math (timed) . . . . . . . 7.1
Math (untimed) . . . . . 16.5
Word Recognition . . . . 11.6
Comprehension . . . . . 12.8

Auditory Dominance . . . Left
Visual Dominance . . . . Left
Manual Dominance . . . Right
Foot Dominance . . . . . Mixed-Right
```

Jenny was excited that Grace was adapting quite well to the left hand, and her writing was becoming neater and faster. Along with the hand-change, Jenny reported her daughter was doing much better emotionally. She was displaying significantly less depression and fewer times of being hard on herself. Surprising both Jenny and Grace were notable improvements in her posture, coordination, endurance, balance, and muscle tone. As a competitive swimmer, those changes truly stood out for Grace. Also, Grace's processing ability and processing rate both improved, which in turn increased her conversational skill and articulation. They were amazed at how all-encompassing the improvements were from merely changing to the correctly designed hand.

### July 2018 2nd Evaluation Notes
Age: 16 years 11 months
Diagnosis: None
Dual Enrollment: High School and Community College

Concerns and Behavior: Much improved in sensitivity, moods, depression, frustration level, good/bad days, phobias. Mild avoidance issues continue. Increased desire to communicate and interact with others appropriately noted.

Crawl: Serialized cross pattern – complete
Creep: Homolateral
Primitive Reflexes (tested) not integrated: Babinski (near complete), Amphibian Moro, STNR complete

```
ADS . . . . . . . . . . . 7
ACWS . . . . . . . . . . 6
VDS . . . . . . . . . . . 6-7
VFD . . . . . . . . . . . 6-7

Math (timed) . . . . . . 7.4
Math (untimed) . . . . . did not complete
Word Recognition . . . . 12.6
```

Auditory Dominance . . . Left
Visual Dominance . . . . Left
Manual Dominance . . . Mixed-Left
Foot Dominance . . . . . Mixed-Right

Grace still found that using her left hand felt awkward and uncomfortable. Though she was using it more and more, she felt a little disillusioned and showed a little attitude. Her hectic schedule allowed little to no downtime, which is critically important. When the central nervous system is undergoing such a considerable amount of reorganization, it dramatically affects the person experiencing the change. Grace was doing a lot with her piano, violin, singing group, worship group, swimming, homeschool, and college. To her seemingly never-ending schedule, she had also added working one day a week at a tutoring center. It stood to reason that negativity had crept in. Grace needed some downtime! We discussed how to ease some of the burdens until the left-hand transition was complete.

### November 2018 3rd Evaluation Notes
Age: 17 years 2 months
Diagnosis: None
Dual Enrollment: High School and Community College

Concerns and Behavior: Still easily distracted, attitude with INP not great

Creep: Serialized cross pattern – complete
Primitive Reflexes (tested) not integrated: Babinski (near complete)
Amphibian complete

ADS . . . . . . . . . . 7
ACWS . . . . . . . . . 7
VDS . . . . . . . . . . 7
VFD . . . . . . . . . . 7, bridge 8

Math (timed) . . . . . . 7.1
Math (untimed) . . . . . 15.4
Word Recognition . . . . 13.8

Auditory Dominance . . . Left
Visual Dominance . . . . Left
Manual Dominance . . . Left-Mixed
Foot Dominance . . . . . Left

March 2019 was Grace's first anniversary of starting an NDApproach program. It would also be her final evaluation, since her neurological organization had finalized. Completing a hand change in one year is quite an accomplishment, and Grace did it! Despite my recommendation to cut back on activities, Grace had maintained her whirlwind schedule. However, as the hand became more natural and controlled, things took off. Her stress level was near non-existent. Grace told me she couldn't believe how great it felt no longer living with the massive, pervasive stress that had always been there and that depression no longer paralyzed her. Jenny noted that Grace was much more flexible with change and unexpected situations. She was delighted her daughter had become cooperative, lost the negative attitude, and no longer had any behavioral issues. Grace displayed poise and confidence. "*She's like a different person*," Jenny said.

### March 2019 4th/Final Evaluation Notes
Age: 17 years 7 months
Diagnosis: None
Dual Enrollment: High School and Community College

Concerns and Behavior: Doing well in classes, all "A's," More relaxed, less stressed with school and other activities. More cooperation, flexibility in attitudes, and behavior. Perfectionism significantly decreased, only seen in a few things. Everything is easier.
"No longer feeling overwhelmed."

Primitive Reflexes (tested) not integrated: None
Babinski complete

```
ADS . . . . . . . . . . . 8
ACWS . . . . . . . . . . 7, bridge 8
VDS . . . . . . . . . . . 7
VFD . . . . . . . . . . . 7, bridge 8

Math (timed)   . . . . . . 8.0
Math (untimed) . . . . .  16.5
Word Recognition . . . .  15.6

Auditory Dominance . . .  Left
Visual Dominance . . . .  Left
Manual Dominance . . .   Left
Foot Dominance . . . . .  Left
```

The sad fact is, too many young people live their lives scrambling to get by – just making it, or not. When life is so hard, how can anyone think or believe for their future? Every person has a calling and destiny, but when life is entangled with struggles, living to get by can lead to mediocrity and keep a person from achieving the future that is possible.

Our current society, and its way of thinking, does not offer hope to the millions of people afflicted with learning disabilities and challenges, it only provides strategies and compensatory techniques. Society lowers expectations and dashes dreams. I listened to one heartbroken mom and dad tell me that the school had said the best hope for their son was to become a truck driver. Now there is nothing wrong with being a truck driver, as it is an admirable occupation requiring a great deal of skill. What's wrong here is that those parents were told that their child had no options and no reason to think or strive for anything different. It's absurd that our culture believes everyone should fit into the restraints of the current definition of success, without realizing the diversity and individuality that exists for each uniquely created person! Each person's goals and accomplishments should be based on his or her life dreams and destiny. We desire to open our children's future by helping them become the best they can be – then, that future offers endless possibilities!

Learning issues need not be life-long sentences handed down to label, limit, and hamper our children (or ourselves). They are conditions with root causes that can be identified, treated, and resolved. Dr. Jan Bedell conducted another study using standardized tests for word recognition, reading comprehension, and math processes. The study, which tested 118 participants, conclusively documented the progress that is achievable with NeuroDevelopmental intervention. The illuminating results detailed in the following graph undeniably offers hope for those who struggle academically. Before starting the NeuroDevelopmental intervention, the participants' average grade-level scores were determined and designated by the chart's dark color bars. The lighter color bars indicate the substantial grade-level increases after only four months of doing an NDApproach program. In our experience, these exciting results are not unique to this study and the benefits will continue on a positive trajectory throughout the neurological re-organizational process and beyond!

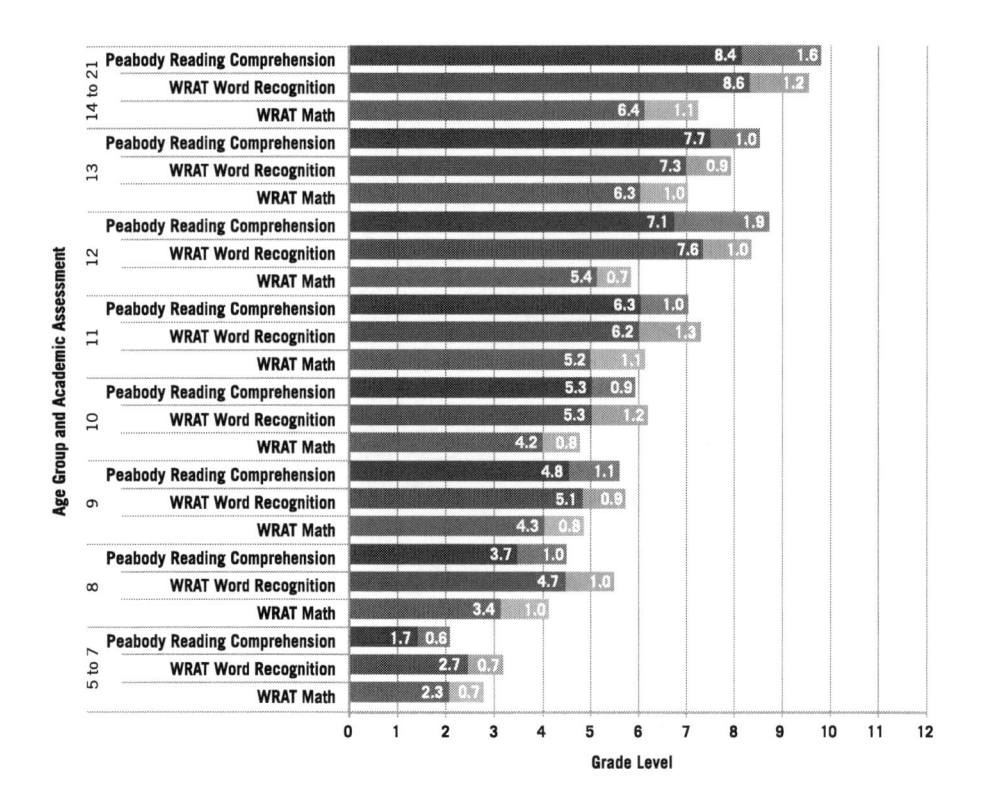

| Age Group | Assessment | Score | |
|---|---|---|---|
| 14 to 21 | Peabody Reading Comprehension | 8.4 | 1.6 |
| | WRAT Word Recognition | 8.6 | 1.2 |
| | WRAT Math | 6.4 | 1.1 |
| 13 | Peabody Reading Comprehension | 7.7 | 1.0 |
| | WRAT Word Recognition | 7.3 | 0.9 |
| | WRAT Math | 6.3 | 1.0 |
| 12 | Peabody Reading Comprehension | 7.1 | 1.9 |
| | WRAT Word Recognition | 7.6 | 1.0 |
| | WRAT Math | 5.4 | 0.7 |
| 11 | Peabody Reading Comprehension | 6.3 | 1.0 |
| | WRAT Word Recognition | 6.2 | 1.3 |
| | WRAT Math | 5.2 | 1.1 |
| 10 | Peabody Reading Comprehension | 5.3 | 0.9 |
| | WRAT Word Recognition | 5.3 | 1.2 |
| | WRAT Math | 4.2 | 0.8 |
| 9 | Peabody Reading Comprehension | 4.8 | 1.1 |
| | WRAT Word Recognition | 5.1 | 0.9 |
| | WRAT Math | 4.3 | 0.8 |
| 8 | Peabody Reading Comprehension | 3.7 | 1.0 |
| | WRAT Word Recognition | 4.7 | 1.0 |
| | WRAT Math | 3.4 | 1.0 |
| 5 to 7 | Peabody Reading Comprehension | 1.7 | 0.6 |
| | WRAT Word Recognition | 2.7 | 0.7 |
| | WRAT Math | 2.3 | 0.7 |

Grade Level

# Mrs. Gordon's Story
*"It's Never Too Late!"*

In August 2017, I met with Carrie, a 72-year-old woman who had lived for years with learning, mental health, and dementia issues. Not happy with the quality of care her mother was receiving where she was living, Carrie's recently retired daughter Toni brought her mother home to live with her. Having seen a friend's daughter's success with the NDApproach, Toni asked whether I thought ND could help her mother or if it was just for children. I responded confidently that it could help anyone, at any age, and with any condition. By the time I met with Carrie, I was sincerely hoping I had not given Toni unrealistic hope. As enthusiastic as I am by the brain's ability to change and improve, I had at the time a limited amount of experience with someone in Carrie's position.

Carrie was very withdrawn, soft-spoken, anxious, and fearful. She barely looked at me; her rounded-in shoulders hunched her forward. Toni had shared with me her mother was withdrawn, depressed, and unmotivated most of the time. I got down on my knees so I could look her in her eyes. I remember asking this precious woman if she would like me to call her Carrie or Mrs. Gordon. She quietly replied, in barely a whisper, "*Mrs. Gordon is fine.*"

In December, after four months of neurodevelopmental intervention and now 73 years old, Mrs. Gordon was undeniably a different woman. The changes brought me to tears. Mrs. Gordon went from needing four to five Pampers a day – she had been entirely incontinent – to using only one at night as a precaution. She was now able to take care of all her toileting needs independently. Doing her ND program had also remarkably improved Mrs. Gordon's memory and recall.

On Thursday of one particular week, Mrs. Gordon had a doctor's appointment with her psychiatrist, who was shocked and amazed at the changes in her and he discussed with Toni and Carrie how well she was doing; the doctor said he had never seen such a transformation. Then, on the following Monday, Mrs. Gordon relayed the entire conversation from Thursday to another doctor she met with regularly. Toni happily remarked her mother had not had that kind of recall in six or more years.

When I first met Mrs. Gordon, she had been detached and reserved. Now, she was much more outgoing and communicative. She talked with better volume, with her shoulders back and her head up. She showed great poise, dignity, and confidence. Upon evaluation, I ascertained that her reading comprehension had increased by two years, and her processing abilities by one developmental year. It was overwhelming to see how this precious woman's quality of life changed for the better.

**It's truly never too late!**

CHAPTER SEVEN

# Bipolar and Anxiety – Gone!

*Soon your rebuilders will come and chase away all those destroying you.*
Isaiah 49:17 – The Living Bible

The Child and Adolescent Bipolar Foundation estimates that three quarters of a million American children and teens may suffer from bipolar disorder, although many have not been diagnosed. My colleagues and I have been waiting for years for a person diagnosed with bipolar to be correctly aligned to their genetic blueprint for handedness – our experience remains that every person with a bipolar diagnosis was working contrary to their brain's genetic dominance. As radical as that sounds, it is a fact. While this may not in fact be the case for all with a bipolar label, we continue to wait to meet the first person who is aligned correctly. Our experience has uncovered a root cause for bipolar symptoms and because our success in addressing those symptoms is remarkable and enduring, we have demonstrated that there is a way to address these issues effectively.

Let's start with some of the data. Following are some official reports on bipolar disorder, from various sources that are cited.

Bipolar disorder, formerly known as manic-depressive illness, is a brain and behavior disorder characterized by severe shifts in a person's mood and energy, making it difficult for the person to function. More than 5.7 million American adults or 2.6 percent of the population age 18 or older in any given year have bipolar disorder. The condition typically starts in late adolescence or early adulthood, although it can show up in children and in older adults. People often live with the disorder without having it properly diagnosed and treated.

While no cure exists for bipolar disorder, it is treatable and manageable with psychotherapy and medications. Mood stabilizing medications are usually the first choice in medication. (Brain and Behavior Research Foundation bbrfoundation.org)

Bipolar disorder, formerly called manic depression, is a mental health condition that causes extreme mood swings that include emotional highs (mania or hypomania) and lows (depression).

Although bipolar disorder is a lifelong condition, you can manage your mood swings and other symptoms by following a treatment plan. In most cases, bipolar disorder is treated with medications and psychological counseling (psychotherapy). (The Mayo Clinic mayoclinic.org)

***Bipolar disorder*** has been diagnosed in children as young as **5**. When young children experience symptoms, this is called early-onset bipolar disorder. (Boston Children's Hospital www.childrenshospital.org)

From webmd.com
The truth is, you have more than one way to manage this illness. Some types of medications can work very well. Your doctor may suggest medicine such as
- Mood stabilizers
- Antidepressants
- Anti-mania drugs

Psychotherapy can also help you keep your symptoms in check. You'll learn how to
- Avoid triggers
- Find support when you need it
- Spot when your symptoms may get worse

From the CDC (www.cdc.gov: April 19, 2019)
7.4% of ***children*** aged 3-17 years (approximately 4.5 million) have a ***diagnosed*** behavior problem. 7.1% of ***children*** aged 3-17 years (approximately 4.4 million) have ***diagnosed anxiety***.

We can see clearly from this that too many children and adults are suffering from the symptoms of bipolar and other deemed "mental health" issues. Many more are crippled from the paralyzing effects of anxiety and are not able to function well. We have heard too many heart-wrenching stories of devastation, hopelessness, and struggle. Parents repeatedly have been told that medication and psychotherapy are the only means of treatment and likely to be lifelong. Once again, millions are afflicted with what I call the "extremes" – extremes in behavior, mood swings, and rage episodes – all undeniably horrifying for families. Understandably, when parents are unable to reason with their child or figure out how to help him or her, they turn to the medical profession for advice and will do anything they can to support their loved one. We have seen another way not just to escape the "nightmare" for these hurting families, but to turn it completely around.

There is good news: We have witnessed these extreme symptoms disappear in many children and adults by organizing the central nervous system neurologically to the correct blueprint for each individual.

## Kay and Carson's Story
*"I thank God often for the ND program!"*

One such family reached out to me with enormous skepticism. Kay and Don had already been through an ND program with their son, Carson, and that program had "graduated" him. His dominance (eye, ear, foot, and hand) had completely lined up to the left side, and his processing was sound. His profile looked perfect on paper. I remember talking with Kay and hearing her anguish when she relayed that something still wasn't right. If Carson was neurologically organized and "complete," why did she still find it necessary to lock him out of the house for protection until Don could get home from work? Carson became so violent that they feared he would do something terrible.

Kay wasn't willing to subject Carson, who had been diagnosed with generalized anxiety disorder, to further intervention without checking it out for herself first, so she scheduled an evaluation with me the following month when I was in her area. Kay also explained that she herself was not coping well with the stress of their situation. Knowing she had mixed dominance herself, Kay understood her emotions would be considerably more stable if she could resolve her neurological disorganization.

Kay was a delightful woman of nearly 52 years old. She and her husband, Don, were quite the team. Don was supportive and calm, precisely what Kay, who had been diagnosed with cyclothymia (a mood disorder with characteristics similar to bipolar) years earlier, needed. Efforts to manage the complex symptoms of that condition included taking four different medications, including anti-depressants, anti-anxiety, and mood-stabilizing drugs. Kay's goals were to become neurologically organized, get off drugs, and to help her son.

When we met, Kay was noticeably stressed and distraught over the situation with Carson. She had done a lot of the lower-level organizational work alongside her son when he did program activities, so her lower-levels were completely organized, and the primitive reflexes I had tested were all integrated. Like many mothers, Kay had also done Carson's sequential processing activities along with him, so her own processing skills were, fortunately, at accelerated levels. Kay did have a bad habit of biting the skin around her fingernails, especially when things weren't going well and also, when she was depressed. My assessment confirmed Kay's mixed dominance. For as long as she could remember, Kay had been left-handed, but she noted that she could eat left or right-handed and often did. Her auditory and visual dominance were primarily right-sided, which meant that since Kay was living left-handed, she was in the subdominant part of her brain all the time, thus allowing emotions to erupt at any given moment. Everything I assessed attested that Kay really should be right-side dominant; she was shocked when I told her my findings, repeating that she had been left-handed as long as she could remember. From her own experience here it began to dawn on Kay that this might also be the case with Carson. After all, he had completed aligning his dominance left, yet nothing had resolved. When you achieve neurological organization, the issues plaguing you dissipate. Her theory proved to be true when I evaluated Carson four months later.

These are Kay's thoughts about the journey she and Carson took:

> "*My son and I did the ND (neurodevelopmental) program together. Eventually, we both had to switch from our left to our right. It was not an easy thing to do, but it has been the single most important therapy we have ever done. We had both been diagnosed with emotional disorders and we were both on medication. At different times, prior to program, we had both tried to get off our medication to no avail. I thank God often for the ND program! We worked VERY HARD. Sometimes when my son would be upset and want to quit because he was just plain tired of the program, I would say, "I understand completely how you feel because I have to do it too, and I do not want to do it either. I know you want to get better and so do I. Let's just creep around the second floor from bedroom to bedroom together." We would help each other with different parts of program and pray that doing ND was what God was going to use to heal us. We have graduated program, and we have been off all medication for over one year and a half, long enough to lose the "LABELS" we were diagnosed with."*

It took Kay only one year to complete her right-side transformation. She marveled at how "in control" she was with her emotions. She was able to think before acting or speaking in anger, her anger didn't escalate anymore, and was surprisingly less frequent. With everything aligned to the right, the right side felt comfortable and natural. Well, except when holding her coffee cup, but she knew that would come, too. Kay shared that she rarely bit the skin around her fingernails anymore, and she was delighted that she could now read while riding in a car. Kay was also ecstatic about how well Carson was doing. His graduation day would come eight months later. Now correctly aligned with the blueprint of his design, he was able to go forward in his life without the crippling effect of his label, all the symptoms that went along with that label, and the side-effects of the medications he no longer needed.

At the evaluation where her son "correctly" graduated from his NDApproach program, Kay shared a distinct memory of driving with her then-seven-year-old son. She remembered looking in her rearview mirror with tears streaming down her face, wondering where her sweet little boy had gone, and questioning what had happened to her baby. Her child had changed into an angry, violent little boy. That was the moment, in my opinion, that his actual genetic coding had surfaced. Carson had already chosen his left hand as his dominant hand, but in actuality, he was genetically coded right-side dominant. Because he had chosen left-side dominance, he now was going against the blueprint of his body, which caused all kinds of emotional and behavioral problems to surface.

A few years later I had a chance to visit with Kay, who insisted that she didn't know how either of them would have gotten through Carson's teenage years had he or she remained the way they were. These are two people of different generations for whom an NDApproach program proved to be an effective remedy for the symptoms that plagued their daily lives and their relationships, and it lasted!

## Nick Bennett's Story
*"No Longer Bipolar"*

When I first met Nick in September 2002, he was nearly 12 years old and living far below his potential. He was barely managing under the weight and symptoms of the ADHD, bipolar, and sensory integration disorder diagnoses he had received. Nick was on several medications, including the heavy-hitter, anti-psychotic ones. He displayed attitude, anxiety, anger, and aggression in most of his waking moments. His dad had given up repairing the holes Nick had made in the walls because Nick would punch them out again within a matter of days. Unable to function in a regular classroom, Nick was in a self-contained class at school. He was depressed, unhappy, and unable to interact appropriately. His processing ability was on the level of a four-year-old, which compounded his problems. His mom, Jenna, confided that because Nick was destructive, she had hidden all the knives and scissors in their home in fear he would hurt someone or himself.

Two years after starting an NDApproach program, Jenna decided to homeschool him in the mornings so they would have the time available for working his ND plan. Too little ND was getting done in the limited time they had in the evenings. Nick was tired, uncooperative, and usually irritable after school, making the stimulation less productive. He still went to school in the afternoon for social interaction, which he was failing miserably, yet Jenna held out hope something would click for him socially. His attitude, which had always been negative, improved considerably with this change. Jenna reinforced her determination to help her son overcome his difficulties when she saw those encouraging changes.

Nick was 15 when the psychiatrist removed the bipolar label, saying that Nick no longer fit the criteria. His parents were thrilled with losing the diagnosis but also knew Nick still had significant issues affecting him. Thankfully, they had been able to reduce all the medications he was taking to only one, a popular ADHD drug. Jenna faithfully kept going, despite some inevitable weariness. Seeing the breakthroughs her son already had achieved was all the motivation she needed.

A few months after Nick was declared free of bipolar, and all the horrific things that came with that label, I could see his neurological picture more clearly and realized he was using the wrong hand for dominance. Nick had worked long and hard to get to where he was, experiencing all the improvements firsthand. Yet, when approached with the new circumstances, he was adamant he would not change his hand dominance.

While things were significantly better overall for Nick, there were still unresolved struggles. One of those struggles, unbeknownst to Jenna and her husband, was at karate. Nick had been in karate since he was five years old, so it was a shock when the headmaster asked Nick to leave a few months before he turned 16. Social issues and lack of self-discipline still were plaguing Nick. Jenna was determined to find a way to convince her son to switch handedness – and she did! During Nick's next evaluation, Jenna laughed at how easy it had been to get him on board with the hand change. She offered to pay him for all his hard work, and that did the trick. Nick began to switch his hand dominance whole-heartedly. It only took eight months to achieve his goal, and the difference in Nick was dramatic. He went from being destructive, angry, rude, disrespectful, and self-loathing to being kind, happy, sweet, and helpful. It was then that Jenna knew their family was finally "*out of the trenches.*" Seeing the transformation in him was all the reward Jenna needed for the years of her dedicated intervention. She said Nick hadn't put a hole in the walls for more than two years, so her husband was finally convinced he could repair and paint them. "*Life is good,*" Jenna had said, and I could see this in Nick's huge smile and sparkling eyes.

## Renee Parks' Story
*"Self-Confident and Mature"*

The Parks family had been told about the NeuroDevelopmental Approach by the online school that oversaw their homeschool efforts with their daughter Renee. The family had seen some dramatic changes in a few of the school's other students who had undergone an ND program and were interested to see if this approach would help Renee.

Renee, officially diagnosed in early 2010, carried labels of separation anxiety disorder, general anxiety disorder, and possible ADHD-Combined. Because Ann Parks operated an in-home daycare, she was able to homeschool Renee. There is no way Renee could have endured being in school with the astronomical levels of stress and anxiety that infiltrated every area of her life. She was one hyperactive, impulsive, destructive, angry, and emotionally charged 10-year-old! Her emotions could flip "on a dime," and her family felt they were always walking on a slippery slope.

Often when someone has severe anxiety, they do self-injurious things as a way of coping – almost like a teapot "spilling over" when its contents are no longer containable. Sadly, Renee had her share of these self-injurious behaviors. For example, Renee bit her fingers until they bled and chewed on her lips and cheeks as well; she also brutally bit her fingernails down past the stubs. Renee was also a very picky eater and overate all the wrong foods when she was upset. Ann was almost in tears when she told me that her daughter had no friends. Renee lacked the skills to understand body language as well as an understanding of personal space.

No one wanted to be around Renee, who always spoke loudly and even louder when she was angry. In fact, Ann noticed the children in her daycare covered their ears and would attempt to get away from Renee. All these things led

Renee to withdraw more and to become even more fearful and rigid. Ann desperately wanted to help her daughter and had no clue how to do so until the school recommended that Renee be evaluated. Tears fell down Ann's face as she related the strain of her daughter's trauma, which ultimately had become the entire family's trauma, as well.

It was quite apparent when Renee was assessed that she had not correctly aligned with the neurological blueprint of her design. Ann was astounded when we explained the genetic coding for dominance. It seemed unfathomable to her that this could cause all of Renee's struggles, and that fixing this alignment was as simple as changing her hand and lining up her ear, eye, and foot dominance correctly.

The next year offered a whirlwind of changes. Within four months of working the ND plan I designed for her, Renee was already in a considerably better place. Ann said that Renee was substantially less needy, she interrupted less and responded more quickly when asked to do something. Even the volume of her voice was quieter, almost down to a reasonable level. What Ann was the most relieved about, she had told me, was that Renee's stress level had reduced considerably. It was unbelievable to Ann that she had seen all this change in just a few short months of starting the ND program to switch Renee's handedness and dominance.

Renee had two more evaluations, attaining her graduation from the NDApproach program in 11 months. During those last seven months of ND, Ann saw a total turnaround for her daughter. Renee's attitude was outstanding. She was no longer embarrassingly rude; she completely understood social cues and her peers' behaviors; and the personal space issues had long been forgotten. Also, long gone were the terrible habits of nail and finger-biting as well as chewing on her lips and cheeks. Picky eating, while not entirely gone yet, had dramatically improved. Ann exuberantly informed me that Renee now had many friends. Her maturity had sky-rocketed and she displayed a new self-confidence that amazed her mother. With Renee's processing skills advanced, her dominance alignment near-complete, stress and anxiety wholly dissipated, she was ready to enter the next stage of her life. Ann excitedly informed me that Renee would be attending sixth grade at a private school in the fall. What had been impossible before ND, was now achievable for Renee. With the impulsivity and hyperactivity gone, as well, Renee could do anything she needed to do. Ann hugged me as she whispered her thanks and agreed that ND is about helping our children be the best of who God created them to be.

That is what the NeuroDevelopmental Approach is all about – helping people get past the symptoms caused by neurological disorganization, symptoms that hold them back from attaining their fullest potential. Most people believe that people with anxiety issues, those with a bipolar or similar label, are trapped in those conditions forever. Medication is frequently the first option offered to families suffering with a child who has symptoms that lead to these labels. We have seen the struggle as one medication then causes a need for another to counteract the effects of the first. We have also seen the experimentation of medication trials. If one is not getting the desired result, wean off that one and try another; all very harsh on an individual.

I'll never forget watching an acquaintance of mine whose arms shook violently. She explained that she couldn't control the shaking caused by changing her meds. Her husband revealed that she paced for hours and hours, unable to stop herself. They both admitted that her anxiety levels were extreme and crippled her ability to function well. Unable to do the simple tasks of keeping the house, she even had given up the gardening she loved. A once happy, effervescent woman had received a bipolar diagnosis at 51 years old and everything declined rapidly from there. She had consented to an evaluation with me and had attempted to do the program I had given her, but she never did do much, if any, of it. After her third evaluation, she quit her program altogether. She decided that medication was more advantageous than changing her hand. Somewhere along that path, she bought into the diagnosis and the label defined her. She went from *"the bipolar"* to *"my bipolar,"* and accepted it as her identity.

## Patty's Journey
*"Bipolar and NeuroDevelopment"*

> *Patty is a phenomenal individual. I am so blessed to have worked with her. She is such an intelligent person but yet she couldn't use that great intelligence because she was not on a strong foundation in her brain. She was truly a house built on sand, double-minded and unstable. She came to me highly intelligent but lacking in the ability to apply that intelligence because of her brain disorganization. She was very strong in her visual*

*abilities but was having a difficult time with her auditory system. She also was not using her dominant hand, which for her was her left. She had no inkling that she was really left-handed when she first arrived at my door. However, as her brain became more organized, she became a much more stable individual, able to handle things that were thrown her way. The same situations can now occur, as they did before she was on program, but now she has the ability to look at them and decide how she is going to handle them instead of letting everything run over her like a tidal wave.*

*And on another note, even her overall countenance and structure were affected. She had bad posture, always having to remind herself to straighten up but now stands straight as an arrow without even thinking about it. She even has nice arches in her feet where she was flat-footed before. Patty's life will never be the same in so many different ways. She is very stable now in all her decision-making and in her ability to live her life day-to-day. Again, it has been a pleasure seeing her change in so many ways. Here is her story, in her own words.*

Faith Haley

My life had come to the point that I had no control over my emotions, my thoughts, and my reactions toward people or circumstances. Looking back, I can't ever remember a time I felt in "control" of myself, and the more daily life I had to "endure," the worse my inner torment became. As a child I always wanted to express my emotions, but even at an early age, I felt that if I truly began expressing the sadness I felt, then I wouldn't be able to stop crying; if I expressed the anger inside, then it could potentially turn into rage; if I expressed happiness and joy, then extreme silliness would set in and I wouldn't know what was appropriate behavior anymore. I never truly grasped emotional balance or social maturity, so my way to cope and "get-by" with social situations and expectations was to cut myself and withdraw inside myself. After I graduated college, though, my behavior and inability to cope with even the simplest of life stresses became increasingly worse, and in my early twenties, after my second trip to a mental hospital, I was diagnosed with bipolar disorder. The rest of my twenties were spent in and out of doctor's offices, mental hospitals, and emergency rooms. Panic attacks were the norm, hallucinations clouded reality, I was unable to have any meaningful relationships, was unable to hold down a part-time job for any length of time and was given the prognosis that my condition could only be "managed," never cured.

I knew God's Word said that I was to "take every thought captive" (2 Corinthians 10:5) and also "[t]he steadfast of mind You will keep in perfect peace because he trusts in You" (Isaiah 26:3), but my very struggle was just that – I was unable to focus my mind or my emotions on anything for any length of time. No matter how hard I tried to be focused and to do "good," I always felt that my mind and body were at the mercy of impulse. The shame I felt was enormous. I came from a good Christian family who loved me and supported every interest I had as a child. I knew I was a Christian and that God's promises to me were His peace, joy, and self-control, but by this point in my life, I considered these promises to only be "religious myths."

In October 2010, I was sitting in church considering suicide. I really wanted to be free from the symptoms and effects of bipolar, but knew the medical community gave no hope for a cure. I was so tired of attending inner-healing and deliverance meetings that never seemed to work for me. I had also lost all hope in God miraculously healing me. Yet as I sat in church that morning, I believed God told me that I needed to share my struggles with a particular person in the church. I thought to myself, "Ok. I can tell her, but I don't know what good it will do because she only works with children who have learning disabilities." Nevertheless, I had nothing to lose. I spoke with her, and we scheduled my first neurodevelopment evaluation for the following month.

I received my first neurodevelopment program at the end of 2010 and continued on program through the beginning of 2012. In all honesty, I thought the activities were absolutely ridiculous and had no understanding of how crawling/creeping on the floor, or spinning in a chair, or even switching to use my left hand, etc. would help my "condition." But, thankfully I had come to the point in my life where I didn't care how ridiculous something seemed; I just wanted to be free.

The success has been miraculous. While on program in 2011, I was able for the first time in my adult life to successfully hold down a part-time job. Since then, I have been able to hold down other part-time jobs and have now "graduated" to working my first full-time job.

Although my healing has been progressive and not the overnight "miracle" so many of us want, I know that God chose neurodevelopment as His pathway for my healing. I am no longer on any medication or under any medical/psychiatric care (this was a process guided by continual wise counsel). I am now able to take thoughts captive and have the ability to have a steadfast mind. I can also choose my thoughts and actions instead of being at the mercy of them.

My family and friends are amazed at the transformation in my life, and this testimony is as much a tribute to their support and love all these years as it is to neurodevelopment. I am thankful and now know that there is and has always been hope for me, as well as for others who are currently struggling with the torments of bipolar. Life is not given to be "managed;" it is given to be lived, and lived more abundantly. There is a way. There is hope and freedom.

# Alec's Journey
*"Severe Anxiety and NeuroDevelopment"*

This story is about our son Alec who is now almost 14 years old. He was a sweet, happy, and very easy baby. Alec had an amazing first five years of school experience starting at preschool, kindergarten, first, second, and third grades. He was an "A" student and good in sports, especially baseball, basketball, and soccer. His teachers and friends adored him for his kindness, good manners, respect for others, and willingness to help.

As his parents, we felt very blessed to have such a good child. In third grade, Alec became an altar boy at our church. It was absolutely wonderful to watch him serve God and the community during Saturday and Sunday masses. He just always had this big smile on his face and was excited about his life.

During 4th grade, at the end of the 1st semester, something happened. Alec suddenly became sad. He developed severe anxiety, terrible panic attacks, and a fearful obsession with the wind. Alec would check his phone several times a day for the weather and wind reports. He would watch television programs that featured weather disasters such as hurricanes. Alec was crying a lot and didn't know why. He couldn't complete a day at school as his mind became paralyzed by fear and panic. Alec was often in the nurse or counselor's offices, trying to find a way to calm down. I was regularly called from the school to come and take Alec home, as he did not feel well. The fear was taking over his life! Alec was no longer able to enjoy sports, friends, or school anymore. He also presented with head and shoulder movement (tics), which would worsen during school hours, basketball games, and while serving at church. Alec would break into tears and leave in the middle of the game or classroom time. Completely losing his motivation and ambition, Alec had quit sports, and his grades had dropped significantly.

Alec tried to explain what he was experiencing to us. He said, "*I sometimes think that I am not me, like there is somebody else in my skin, like I am out of my own skin, like it's not me...*" Many evenings, he would cry and ask, "*Will I ever be happy again? Why do I feel this way?*"

Our hearts had broken into pieces. As parents, these were painful and terrifying moments of our lives. I tried to hide my tears so he wouldn't see them. I needed to be strong for Alec, and I knew the strength could only come from God. We knew medication would not fix what was going on. We knew only God had the answer. We knew we had to trust in Him and believe He would bring the healing. We prayed. The pain we carried in our hearts was unbearable. We just wanted our son to be happy again.

One day after Sunday mass, one of our parishioners approached me and asked about Alec. She said she noticed his behavior while he was serving, and she thought we might like to see the same person her son had seen for years. I believed this was our answer to our prayers. I knew deep inside that this lady was sent from up above to show us direction. I called the next day to schedule an appointment with Linda.

What happened next is a pure miracle. After the first four weeks of being on the program designed by Linda (which included changing Alec's hand dominance), we noticed small improvements. As the weeks went by, those small improvements got bigger and bigger. Today, I am so happy to say that our boy is back. Alec is happy again, and you should see his smile! His symptoms are gone. He's back to sports, and his grades are up. He is a straight "A" student and a winner of the "Student of the Month" award in 7th grade, which he just completed. We are grateful that Alec is also back serving as an altar boy, which he had also given up on due to severe anxiety, fear, and tics.

We believed it was God's plan for us to meet with Linda. She is an extremely talented, educated, knowledgeable, and caring specialist that we were blessed to work with. The very first moment we met her, we knew she was the one. There was an immediate peace that we felt during that initial assessment. There are no words to describe the relief we've had. We deeply believe God uses her to heal people. Thank You!

Beyond drugs, families are also sent to psychotherapy, behavioral therapy, and family support groups so they can learn to cope, manage, and then, sadly, to accept the situation. It's important to remember that symptoms surface from an underlying root cause and discovering and rooting out those causes should be the first and foremost treatment.

*Eliminating anxiety and bipolar symptoms can happen.*

*There is hope!*

CHAPTER EIGHT

# The NDApproach with Adults

*I am focusing all my energies on this one thing:*
*Forgetting the past and looking forward to what lies ahead…*
Philippians 3:13 – New Living Translation

The primary focus of *Hope And A Future* has been working with children – the heartbeat of our work. However, I cannot encourage adults enough to embrace the NeuroDevelopmental Approach for themselves. It is never too early or too late for someone to improve his or her life through the NDApproach.

Working with adults is an honor, but it has not been my favorite part of this work, for several reasons. The failure rate is high because adults are so very busy. They have work, home, family, and a myriad of responsibilities. Many adults have come to me stating that they felt like they were "falling apart," like they were "treading water" every day and were barely getting by. Some resorted to medications, which only sapped their energy and stamina even more. Since the NDApproach changed my life as an adult, I have chosen to continue to see adults who seek this course for their own lives, despite the high failure rate. Every adult evaluation is an offering of hope to them that things can be different and that their life can be better. Recently, I was surprised at my excitement when I noticed I had several new adults to see that week. The failure rate has declined considerably and working with adults has become a sheer joy!

We also have noted that adults who are the most desperate somehow find their way to the success of completing an NDApproach program. We have seen examples of many adults in the previous chapters, and I applaud their tenacity; it is not easy for adults to make the changes that are necessary to organize their central nervous system. Their inefficiencies have been "with" them for a much longer time than those in children, which means that the "muscle memory" is more locked-in. Habits have been established for a long time. The adults who have succeeded in this approach have never regretted the time and effort it took to complete the NDApproach. Each one has joyfully reported how peaceful life has become for them since they have become neurologically organized and their dominance is complete. They feel a fresh vigor and vitality. Hope for their future has returned.

# Jake's Story
*"Journey from Struggling to Productive and Well-Equipped"*

Jake started his NDApproach program as a teenager. He had so many labels attached to and limiting him. He had been diagnosed with:
- ADHD (attention deficit, with hyperactivity disorder)
- OCD (obsessive-compulsive disorder)
- ODD (oppositional defiant disorder)
- Dyslexia (disability affecting reading, writing, and spelling)
- Scotopic's sensitivity syndrome (light sensitivity)
- Occulomotor dysfuntion (uncoordinated eye muscle movement)
- PDD (Pervasive developmental disorder)
- Asperger's syndrome (an Autism spectrum disorder)
- Latent growth (below the curve for typical growth)

The labels placed on him had done absolutely nothing over the years to help him. He was frustrated, angry, and unable to keep up in school. Jake was going against his genetic coding and should have been left-side dominant. However, he resisted changing his dominance and doing an NDApproach program. Jake's parents decided after coming for a few years, that if he was not willing to do the work there was no reason for them to keep bringing him for re-evaluations. The little amount of program Jake had accomplished had been helpful and he was able to finish high school and graduate. The family was relieved that he had obtained his diploma, but struggles were still in abundance. Until the root cause of the struggles are discovered and then fixed, the individual will live in their created world of coping and compensatory techniques. Jake was twenty years old when he finally realized that it was just too much work being neurologically disorganized. The daily battles of compensating that he faced led Jake back to the NDApproach and as an adult he paid for the evaluations himself. It took a little over a year to switch Jake's dominance from right to left-sided and the changes were remarkable. Jake now has thinking and reasoning skills that had always eluded him; his excessive, inappropriate anger and frustration are gone, and he is able to be more productive and successful at work. He is happy, interactive, engaging and well-equipped to take on college, which is now in his plans. Jake had one final evaluation that confirmed his neurological organization was complete. His future and its full potential had been opened to him.

## Sharon's Family
*"Gone Are the Days of Frustration"*

The journey of Sharon's family is another success story. I remember that she smiled across the table from me after we had "graduated" her third, and final, child from an NDApproach program. *"Now,"* she said, *"It is my turn."* She had seen how organizing her children's central nervous systems had paved the way to ease in school, excellent grades, and social maturity. Faithfully working with her children for the previous six years had shown her the value of the NDApproach. She knew that improving her children's processing and organizing their brains had, in turn, made learning easy for them. They no longer labored for hours over homework and gone were the days of frustration over "not getting it." Before beginning her own journey, Sharon had decided she was ready to make her world easier and more efficient, and that is exactly what she did!

Sharon smiled brightly as she sat across the table from me for the last time. It was her very own day of "graduation" from the NDApproach. She marveled at the changes in her life since beginning her ND "plan of action." Her eyes sparkled as she told me her vision was so clear; she no longer needed to use reading or distance glasses. She was amazed that the arches in her feet had developed, as she had been flat-footed her entire life. Her posture was perfect and gone were the days of having to continually remind herself to stand straight. Sharon is more relaxed, organized and has greater retention of information. She laughed as she said, *"Perhaps my husband will realize it is his turn for an ND plan."*

## Connie's Story
*"From Hyper-Organized to a New Calm"*

Connie was one who overcompensated for her inefficiencies. Everything had to have its place. It was amazing how Connie had guided her four sons through NDApproach programs, as highly neurologically disorganized as she was. One time when I visited her home, I realized how she managed everything. In order to compensate for her neurological disorganization, Connie's life was "hyper-organized." Everything had a place and was in order. She had an amazing labeling system and "Post-It Notes" were stuck on cabinet doors, the refrigerator, and countertops. Connie had cubicle shelving throughout the rooms in their home, further helping to sort and place objects. Nothing could be out of place or she would feel sudden "chaos" overwhelm her.

Her sons' programs called for using the tactile stimulation gloves twice per day. She could have used one pair of gloves for each boy and each frequency of stimulation. Or, she could have had four pairs of gloves with each son having his own pair. Instead, Connie had eight pairs of gloves – one pair of gloves for each repetition on each program. Every set of program activities Connie did was organized into gallon-sized plastic bags. Throughout the day Connie progressed through each son's program, working her way through the plastic bags. When the last bag was removed from the "working" bin, the program had been completed for that day and all plastic bags were back in their respective cubicles awaiting the next day's start.

After Connie became organized herself, through doing an NDApproach program, the changes in her life were amazing. She happily talked about how she could simultaneously stir dinner and talk on the phone for the first time. Multi-tasking had previously been impossible for her. Connie is also amazed at how light no longer bothers her and wants the curtains pulled wide open rather than drawn shut. Her Post-It Notes disappeared and menu planning became a joy, rather than drudgery. Her family has commented on how Connie smiles and sings more. The boys' roughhousing and spirited play could no longer drive her "to the edge." She also noticed how her new calmness enabled her to enjoy her children more. Connie's husband was very delighted with his "new wife."

The NDApproach produces life-altering changes that are priceless! You cannot buy neurological organization or re-organization. You cannot use medication to achieve neurological organization. You can achieve it, though, with carefully calculated activities, determination, perseverance, and believing in yourself.

CHAPTER NINE

# Transformations!

*Let God transform you into a new person by changing the way you think.*
Romans 12:2 – New Living Translation

I have wished that others could see through my eyes and witness the incredible transformations we have seen and taken part in. It is radical to say dyslexia, bipolar, ADD, ADHD, and the other learning challenges can disappear merely by correctly aligning the brain's natural dominance – but that is our experience. Privileged to have been part of thousands of life-changing neurological organizations for three decades, I have witnessed these remarkable changes routinely – but it's never ordinary. Every transformation is an extraordinary miracle for each person and for his or her family.

In this final chapter, we share "snapshots" and "mini-snapshots" of persons who found their lives radically improved by neurologically organizing their central nervous systems to the pattern genetically wired in their brains. Helping our children and loved ones become the best God created them to be is the heart desire of our *Hope And A Future* families. Thank you for letting me share your journey.

## SNAPSHOTS

### *Anna: 13 years old*
Anna's aunt had come to a conference where I was speaking, hoping to get some answers for concerns regarding her son's learning challenges. As she listened to me explaining about the brain and how someone who is not neurologically organized "lives" in his or her emotions, Anna's aunt realized that this information was the key to her niece's extreme behaviors. Anna's aunt was cautiously optimistic and couldn't wait to tell her sister that there were reasons why Anna was so out-of-control and that she didn't have to stay that way. There was hope for Anna!

> Initial Evaluation Notes:
> Anna is a sweet girl whose stress levels are alarmingly high, and she displays severe mood swings that leave the family feeling they are on a continual rollercoaster ride. Constantly in crisis mode, and experiencing out of control emotions, Anna can be confrontational, often irrational, and very loud. The extreme circumstances she lives with has caused her to be hospitalized twice for inpatient treatment, thus throwing

the entire family into crisis mode. Despite the unpredictable and intense shifts in behavior and mood, Anna has a loving nature and desperately wants to have friends and good relationships with friends and family alike. Her actions act like roadblocks, keeping her from seeing those desires materialize.

Diagnosis:
Disaggregated mood disorder
ADHD
Anxiety
Schizophrenia
Intellectual delay

History:
Hip dysplasia relocation - 9 months
Broken left arm – 4 years
Facial plastic surgery after trauma from a fall – 9 years
Crawling (never) Creeping (never) Walking (22 months)

ND Evaluation:
Left-handed – the blueprint presented right-side dominant
Ear dominance firmly right
Eye dominance primarily left
Foot dominance completely right
Fine motor delays
Processing significantly low
Primitive reflexes active
Lower-level organization insufficient
Neurological organization incomplete

The Strategy:
Strengthen and complete lower-level organization
Integrate primitive reflexes
Align to right-side dominance
Increase processing
Organize the central nervous system

The Transformation: 11 months of ND (ND program ongoing)
75% right-side dominant
Processing increased
Stress levels significantly lower, weeks of no stress noted
Able to control emotions, no hysteria or dramatic highs and lows
Stable, good relationships have developed
Neurological Organization – in the process of completion

## **Mitch: 50 years old**

Mitch came for an evaluation at the encouragement of his wife. He was highly successful personally and professionally, but she felt there were brain stimulation activities that could make things even better for her husband. Mitch forgets things often, is unable to listen to multiple directions at a time and takes a long time to process information. He decided to do an NDApproach program after his wife agreed to do something she had been contemplating for herself. In the end, they both had a win!

### Initial Evaluation Notes:
Very healthy and active. Mitch enjoys mountain biking, skiing, and Cross-Fit. No sleep concerns. Struggles with jumping into ongoing conversations. His goals are to improve processing speed and ability, memory, and increase his ability to listen.

### History:
Broken arm – 18 years
Knee surgery: ACL – 45 years
MRI to determine the cause of his "brain fog" (nothing found)
Partially torn rotator cuff – right shoulder
Crawling (unknown) creeping (unknown) walking (unknown)

### ND Evaluation:
Right-handed – blueprint has not established
Eye and ear dominance firmly left
Foot dominance primarily left
Processing low
Visual inefficiencies
Lower-level organization mildly insufficient
Neurological organization incomplete

### The Strategy:
Reinforce and complete lower-level organization
Determine the blueprint (subsequently determined left-side)
Align to left-side dominance
Increase processing
Eliminate visual inefficiencies
Organize the central nervous system

### The Transformation: 12 months of ND (graduated)
100% left-side dominant
Processing increased by two developmental years
Visual inefficiencies – gone!
Memory – excellent
Multi-tasking ability – excellent
Listening to multi-step directions – excellent
Communicating at work and home – excellent
Calmer, increased focus and attention
Neurological Organization – Complete!

At his final evaluation, Mitch commented, "*I was surprised how much everything improved. I had thought things were going considerably well for me. I only did this for my wife, but I am grateful I did. I am really amazed how much better things have gotten. Across the board, everything is quicker, easier, and more comfortable. I am amazed at how much stronger my conversational ability is and how much more relaxed I am.*"

## *Jen and Tracey*

When Jen and Tracey's mother heard me speak at a *Teach Them Diligently* homeschool convention, she knew she finally had found answers for two of her children. Homeschooling eight children, over a thirty-year span, made this mom quite the veteran at teaching. Jen and Tracey, however, had her baffled with their learning challenges. Years of tutoring, learning "tricks," and various reading programs had made little difference. Persevering for years, and never giving up, she was ecstatic finally to have the clear-cut answers she had been seeking.

Tears were in her eyes at the first evaluation as she listened to me explain the girls' results. After learning all the "root causes" of the issues, she smiled and said that throughout all the years of not knowing how to help them learn, she had never doubted that her girls were brilliant. The problem was she just couldn't figure out how to unlock the learning obstacles that had long kept Jen and Tracey far below their capabilities. She now knew exactly what to do, and she couldn't wait to get her girls started on their ND program.

## *Jen: 17 years old*

Initial Evaluation Notes:
Learning struggles abounded from the very beginning. After trying various methods and phonics programs, Jen finally learned to read in 4th grade. Even once reading, comprehension was difficult; math was near impossible. She was always two to three years behind grade level in her subjects, which made her very self-conscious. Jen developed a strategy for joking as a means to hide her self-consciousness from others. She appears confident on the surface, yet there is a significant struggle going on underneath. Jen summed up her situation quite succinctly, "*I am sometimes, no, often confused.*"

History:
Nursing difficulties for the first six weeks
Episodes of passing out when upset (reason unknown)
Wisdom teeth extracted – 16 years
Crawl (unknown) creep (unknown) Walk (10 months)

<u>ND Evaluation:</u>
Right-handed – blueprint presented left-side dominant
Eye and ear dominance firmly left
Foot dominance primarily left
Processing low
Lower-level organization insufficient
Neurological organization incomplete

<u>The Strategy:</u>
Reinforce and complete lower-level organization
Align to left-side dominance
Increase processing
Organize the central nervous system

<u>The Transformation:</u> 8 months of ND (graduated)
100% left-side dominant
Processing increased by one developmental year
Academics going well
Successfully doing dual high school and college credit classes
CLEP test preparation successfully underway
Confusion – gone!
Neurological Organization – Complete!

## *Tracey: 9 years old*

<u>Initial Evaluation Notes:</u>
Learning struggles, like her sister, were seen from the very beginning in Tracey. She has a challenging time with memory, reading, letter reversals, and writing words backwards. A precious, soft-spoken girl, Tracey shuts down when confused or embarrassed. Despite being a bit stubborn, she tries hard to please and gets along well with everyone.

<u>History:</u>
Crawl (unknown) Creep (6 months) Walk (11-12 months)

<u>ND Evaluation:</u>
Right-handed – blueprint presented left-side dominant
Ear dominance firmly left
Eye and foot dominance primarily left
Visual inefficiencies
Processing significantly low
Primitive reflexes active
Lower-level organization poor, midline crossing difficult
Neurological organization incomplete

<u>The Strategy:</u>
Strengthen and complete lower- and mid-level organization
Align to left-side dominance

Integrate primitive reflexes
Improve visual inefficiencies
Increase processing
Organize the central nervous system

The Transformation: 48 months of ND (graduated)
100% left-side dominant
Processing increased by nearly three developmental years
Academically doing great!
Visual inefficiencies – gone!
Neurological Organization – Complete!

Tracey had a slower journey with her NDApproach program than her sister did. Numerous family events (weddings to plan, new grandchildren to welcome, and graduations to celebrate) understandably disrupted Tracey's ND program. Knowing she was young and there would be plenty of time ahead for working with her youngest daughter, Tracey's mom had not been worried by the delays. Having witnessed Jen's successful completion and transformation, she knew it would be just a matter of waiting for the right time with Tracey. Mom was wise not to push when those life events happened, and her faithfulness in waiting paid off. When things had settled down, and the time available opened up, Tracey sailed through her ND program successfully to completion.

I'll never forget the last time I met with Tracey and her mom. As I worked with Tracey that morning, it became evident that this would be her final evaluation. The astute, mature, confident, and well-spoken young woman sitting with me no longer exhibited any of the issues that had concerned her parents for years. I witnessed, utterly amazed once again, a life transformed.

### *Hayden: 4 years old*

I could hear the desperation in her voice the first time I talked with Hayden's mom. It is something I often hear when talking with moms who are desperately trying to help their child. His mom said that they had done "everything" and spent a small fortune pursuing numerous treatments. When a friend told her about the NDApproach, she knew this was something different, and it made perfect sense that the brain played a crucial role in her son's dysfunction.

> Initial Evaluation Notes:
> Even though Hayden is only four years old, his parents are exhausted with all they have to do to keep up with his never-ending needs. He has gut issues, parasite concerns, metal toxicity, and numerous food allergies. Hayden craves carbohydrates,

hotdogs are the only meat allowed to pass his lips, and no foods could touch each other or be blended. His constant "scripting" is bittersweet in contrast to the days they agonized that he might never talk.

Diagnosis:
PDD-NOS: An Autism spectrum disorder

History:
Traumatic birth
ABA Therapy – 2 years
Auditory Integration Training
Perseveration, stimming behaviors, massive meltdowns and tantrums

ND Evaluation:
Right-handed – too early for his blueprint to establish
Sensory issues with sound, touch, odors, foods, and eating
Sensory stimulation behaviors and scripting
No social awareness or conversational ability
Short attention span, impulsive, emotional, easily frustrated
Visual inefficiencies
Low processing, few self-help skills, behavioral concerns
Lower-level organization incomplete

The Strategy:
Implement our behavior program before starting his INP
Strengthen and complete lower-level organization
Input sensory activities to normalize sensory dysfunction
Teach him to play interactively and with toys
Teach him to read
Increase processing ability
Eliminate underlying visual inefficiencies
Organize the central nervous system

The Transformation: 84 months of ND (graduated)
Right-side dominance near-complete (will continue post-graduation)
Lower-level organization complete
Sensory dysfunctions normalized
PDD-NOS – gone!
Interactions and play established and improving
Processing above average
Visual inefficiencies – gone!
Neurological organization in the process of completion

This sweet note came in from his mother several years later:

*Dearest Linda – Where would we be without you and ND?*

*Hayden is now a freshman at a college prep private high school. His grades are excellent, he just made the JV basketball team (as a freshman), and his interaction with students and teachers are great. Hayden has absolutely no problem reading all the complex social cues and situations. He has made many friends and is having so much fun despite the rigorous academics. Sometimes I still can't believe he used to be on the spectrum. I remember doing two or more ND sessions/day for one to two hours each, five days a week for so many years, but it seems like another lifetime ago!*

## Carley: 12 years old

There are seven children in Carley's family; she is the second. Her mother told me that Carley had struggled since the beginning of kindergarten, and it was particularly painful to see her struggle while witnessing her siblings' effortless academic success. With Carley soon entering sixth grade, Mom's concerns were growing exponentially, and she had increased her research on what to do. That was when she heard about The NDApproach, and then discovered that I would be in her area the following week.

Initial Evaluation Notes:
Carley excels in sports, Lacrosse being her favorite. She is fast – has excellent skills and determination. Carley's learning challenges don't appear to exist on the playing field. In school, however, she is quiet, withdrawn, and lacks confidence as it is quite apparent to others that she cannot keep up.

Diagnosis:
No official diagnosis received, although Carley's mother said there is no doubt Carley would be labeled with dyslexia if tested. Both parents declined to go the route of a label that could follow their daughter for life. Both of Carley's parents worked in special education, which is what propelled them to keep seeking answers for their daughter's struggles rather than learning to live with them.

History:
Crawl (never) Creep (never) Walk (10 months)

ND Evaluation:
Right-handed – blueprint presents left-side dominant
Eye dominance firmly left
Ear and foot dominance mixed
Processing mildly low

Primitive reflexes active
Lower-level organization incomplete

The Strategy:
Strengthen and complete lower-level organization
Integrate primitive reflexes
Align dominance to the left
Increase processing
Organize the central nervous system

The Transformation: 8 months of ND (graduated)
Left-side dominance 100% complete
Processing superior
Making friends and more comfortable around people
Dyslexia symptoms – gone!
Neurological Organization – complete!

## *Martin and Gregory*

Martin and Gregory are the youngest of three brothers. Martin's initial evaluation was done remotely, via computer. When I had finished explaining the results of his assessment to his mother, she quietly asked if I had any other times available. The more I had uncovered the root causes negatively affecting Martin, the more she realized her youngest son needed ND intervention, too. She was so thankful I could see him the next day so that she could get started with both boys.

## *Martin: 8 years old*

Initial Evaluation Notes:
Because their oldest son is quick to learn and figure things out, Martin is a complete puzzle to his parents. They have to coach him through simple tasks an 8-year-old should be able to do, such as getting dressed, going to the bathroom, and other, necessary daily living routines. He is unwilling to do schoolwork and becomes the "funny guy" as a means for covering up his inability to keep up with his classmates. It is his emotional outbursts, though, that cause the most hindrance for the family. Martin is easily frustrated, explodes in tantrums often, and has very little patience. He is disobedient, contrary, and often wants to dominate when playing with others.

History:
High fever – 9 days old. Hospitalized three days (cause unknown)
Crawl (never) Creep (never) Walk (18 months)

ND Evaluation:
Right-handed – blueprint not established
Ear dominance mixed

Eye dominance primarily right
Foot dominance primarily left
Lower-level organization insufficient
Processing deficient and excruciatingly slow
Primitive reflexes active
Neurological organization incomplete

The Strategy:
Strengthen and complete lower-level organization
Integrate primitive reflexes
Use both left and right hands until the blueprint establishes
Subsequently, the blueprint presented right-side dominant
Increase processing
Complete neurological organization

The Transformation: 16 months of ND (graduated)
100% right-side dominant
Processing improved 18 months developmentally
Academic success!
Math increased three years
Word recognition increased seven years
Reading comprehension increased five years
Anger, tantrums, outbursts, overreactions, and complaints – gone!
Happier, confident, mature, obedient
Enjoys school and learning – the "funny guy" disappeared
Neurological Organization – Complete!

## *Gregory: 5 years old*

Initial Evaluation Notes:
An extremely nervous and anxious little boy, Gregory becomes very stressed when he is not at home with his immediate family. Continually clinging to his mother, he primarily watches from the sidelines or shuts down completely, whenever anyone beyond his immediate family is present or when they are all at church or a friend's house. Gregory has no friends or interaction with peers, which is a significant concern for his parents.

There are very few foods that Gregory will eat because of his extreme pickiness and being bothered by odors, tastes, and textures. Sensory in other avenues, as well, Gregory craves hugs, is always heavily leaning into his parents, and cannot tolerate anything wet or sticky.

Additionally, Gregory is driving his parents crazy by continually asking the same questions over and over, even though he knows the answer to every repetitive question. Often, Gregory goes non-verbal for long periods due to his frustration over his inability to express himself.

History:
Traumatic birth
Crawl (never) Creep (never) Walk (17 months)

ND Evaluation:
Right-handed – blueprint not established
Refused processing games: follows two-three step directions at home
Lower-level insufficient
Neurological organization incomplete

The Strategy:
Strengthen and complete lower-level organization
Use both right and left hands until the blueprint establishes
Subsequently, the blueprint presented right-side dominant
Increase processing
Complete neurological organization

The Transformation: 16 months of ND (unofficially graduated)
Hand and foot – 100% right-side-dominant
Ear and eye dominance primarily right
Lower-level organization mildly insufficient
Processing increased two developmental years
Recent interest in reading noted
Has friends!
Plays at friends' houses, even able to stay overnight
Interaction and play appropriate
Neurological Organization – on its way to completion

Gregory's parents decided to discontinue Gregory's ND program when Martin graduated from his ND plan. They were ecstatic with Gregory's progress and the incredible breakthroughs he was having socially. They were thrilled and grateful, as they shared with me how Gregory had "finally emerged." Martin and Gregory's parents felt confident they could steer their youngest son through the rest of his journey to achieving neurological organization on their own. I agreed with them wholeheartedly and had no doubt they would see it through to completion.

## *Janice: 36 years old*
We had worked with several of Janice's children after which it was finally her turn to come in for an NDApproach evaluation. She had self-designed a program for herself, based on what she had learned with her children and had come to realize her blueprint was left-side-dominant. Being a busy homeschooling mother of seven, Janice decided she needed an exact plan-of-action and not the patchwork program she had put together. Even though I

had given my input for what she could do based on what she told me, a full assessment was important because too many underlying root causes could go unnoticed and left untreated, hampering progress. Janice knew a comprehensive evaluation was the only way to ensure optimal results for the time and energy she was investing.

Initial Evaluation Notes:
Janice is excited about the increased organization skills she is experiencing since changing to left-hand dominance. It is giving her the motivation to continue, as well as encouragement that her emotional outbursts and shutdowns will subside.

History:
Forceps delivery – 37 weeks
Ear infections, allergies
Tonsillectomy – 4 years
Kidney stones – ongoing
Recurring bouts of depression since 12 or 13 years old
First concerns: 30 years – tired all the time, disorganized, emotional
All manual dominant hand function (Right), except for eating (Left)
Crawl (unknown) Creep (unknown) Walk (unknown)

ND Evaluation:
Right-mixed dominance – Blueprint presented left
Ear dominance primarily right
Eye dominance firmly left
Foot dominance completely right
Processing fluctuates depending on emotions
Easily stressed, overwhelmed, resulting in frequent "shut-downs"
Angry, outbursts, feeling out of control
Crawl unobserved, creeping in a homolateral pattern
Neurological organization incomplete

The Strategy:
Strengthen and complete lower-level organization
Align to left-side dominance
Increase processing
Organize the central nervous system

The Transformation: Seven months of ND (ND program ongoing)
Hand dominance primarily left, progressing nicely
Ear dominance mixed, transition to the left progressing well
Foot dominance entirely right, not being worked on
No longer needs naps, significantly less tired overall
Depression – gone!
Organizational skills and ability substantially improved

Less anger (increased anger noted with too much right-hand use)
Emotions much more even-keel
Improved focus
No longer stressed, overwhelmed and never shuts down

Janice took a long break from having evaluations. Every time she quit working on left-side dominance, organizational abilities would disappear and left-hand dominance slipped. Fortunately, depression never returned, and her short-temper and anger were never as bad as they had been initially. When she was 40 years old, Janice returned for her third evaluation and was determined to see her journey through to completion. She had experienced first-hand that not ensuring that her dominance was "locked-in" had kept her from achieving her full potential.

The Transformation: 12 months after returning to ND
Left-hand dominance nearly complete
Ear dominance 100% left
Foot dominance 90% left
Lower-level organization complete
Left hand feeling more natural and automatic
Conversational language improved
She is doing exceptionally well in every area of her life!

Janice had scheduled herself for another evaluation to make sure everything tested 100% left, and her neurological organization was utterly locked-in, but that has not yet occurred. As with most busy families there is always something else to do, and she had graduations and weddings to plan. I would be shocked if Janice did not complete her transformation, as she was one determined lady two years ago – the last time I saw her.

### *Roger: 11 years old*
Having witnessed the excellent results of her friend's son, Roger's mom became intrigued by the NeuroDevelopmental Approach. The two boys were very similar, including their sneakiness in hiding in the pantry to binge on snacks meant to be occasional treats. When she had heard this boy was no longer experiencing learning issues and had even quit sneaking snacks and eating sugar straight from the canister, she was ready to give the NDApproach a try.

Initial Evaluation Notes:
It is easy for adults and children alike to pass by Roger in a group setting. He is quiet, soft-spoken, and doesn't make eye contact. He hates speaking in front of a

group even more than being in a group. If there was a choice between engaging with people or electronics, electronics always won. His mother said that his desire to withdraw and hide severely limited his life.

Diagnosis:
Speech delayed – 5 years

History:
Explosiveness, anger, and disorganization.
Crawl (8 months) Creep (9-10 months) Walk (12 months)

ND Evaluation:
Right-handed – blueprint presented right-side dominant
Ear and foot dominance thoroughly mixed
Eye dominance mixed, slightly more to the left
Processing low
Visual inefficiencies
Doesn't like to read
Toe-walker
Neurological organization incomplete

The Strategy:
Reinforce and complete lower-level organization
Align to right-side dominance
Increase processing
Eliminate visual inefficiencies
Organize the central nervous system

The Transformation: 24 months of ND (graduated)
100% right-side dominant
Processing increased by two developmental years
Visual inefficiencies – gone!
Academically doing well! Reading for pleasure!
Giving presentations in front of groups confidently
Enjoying interaction and engagement with peers
Toe-walking – gone!
Neurological Organization – Complete!

### *Ashleigh: 8 years old*

She cries every school day, Ashleigh's mother told me. The tears would start silently, cascading down her cheeks, breaking her momma's heart. She didn't know why learning was so hard for her daughter, but she often would put the books away and tell her they would try again tomorrow. Each "tomorrow" was never any better. Having learned about the NDApproach through her homeschool association, Ashleigh's mother had tears of her own, realizing that there was a way to get to the root of Ashleigh's struggles and help her overcome her learning failures.

### Initial Evaluation Notes:
Ashleigh was born with deficient blood sugar levels, resulting in multiple surgeries and five months of her first year of life in the hospital. Nearly all of her first two years were spent managing prolonged periods of profound hypoglycemia, with her parents profusely praying to prevent the brain and organ damage that often accompany this anomaly. Her parents are so thankful that no impairment occurred, but they have concerns regarding Ashleigh's many learning struggles, immaturity, and emotionality. Her mom says Ashleigh feels deeply, remembers hurts sadly, and knows exactly how to push her sibling's button and act as though she hadn't.

### Diagnosis:
Hyperinsulinism – a rare genetic disorder

### History:
Profound hypoglycemia
Chronic ear infections
Six surgeries
Mild tonic-clonic seizures
Crawl (7 months) Creep (9 months) Walk (12 months)

### ND Evaluation:
Right-handed – blueprint presents left-side dominant
Ear and Eye dominance primarily left
Foot dominance completely right
Processing low
Highly distractible, bothered by sounds
Motion sickness
Visual inefficiencies
Primitive reflexes active
Lower-level organization incomplete

### The Strategy:
Strengthen and complete lower-level organization
Integrate primitive reflexes
Align dominance to the left
Eliminate sound sensitivity
Increase processing
Eliminate visual inefficiencies
Organize the central nervous system

### The Transformation: 12 months of ND (graduated)
Left-side dominance 100% complete
Lower-level organization – complete

>   Primitive reflexes near complete
>   Processing superior
>   Sound sensitivity, motion sickness, and distractibility – gone!
>   Visual inefficiencies – gone!
>   Neurological Organization – complete!

Ashleigh happily reported to me that she had gone from the weakest basketball player on the team to the most proficient. It was exciting to watch the once-emotional young girl become happy, confident, and able to control her emotions. She still had some overreactions and was too hard on herself, but most of those lingering concerns will fade away as the newly established dominance becomes solidified.

Four years later, I received a note from Ashleigh's mother. She was extremely concerned regarding her daughter's decline in emotional stability – her distractibility issues had returned and schoolwork was suddenly taking excessively long to get through. I suspected her dominance had slid, and we both agreed it was important for Ashleigh to have another evaluation. The assessment revealed that dominance indeed was the culprit, with her ear, eye, and hand dominance all shifting back partially to the right.

>   The Transformation: three months after returning to ND
>   Left-side dominance 100% completely locked in
>   Attention span and focus – excellent
>   Inappropriate emotional responses – gone!
>   Maturity significantly increased
>   Showing substantially more initiative and discipline
>   Loves school and gets through it quickly

## *Jackson: 8 years old*

Our son Michael, an NDApproach professional in his own right, had evaluated Jackson and told me that he was exceptional at school socially and in sports, but not in learning. Happy as his parents were about his social and sports success as well as the school's accommodation of Jackson, his parents didn't quite know how to help him progress with the learning. While they had no desire to homeschool Jackson, they were ready to take on "ND" to help him get past his learning challenges.

>   Initial Evaluation Notes:
>   Jackson's dominance is seriously in question. He writes, draws, and brushes his teeth with his left hand, but uses his right hand to eat, throw a ball, and comb his hair. He struggles to get his words out, is unable to adequately verbalize or

communicate with a basic vocabulary. His parents' goals are for him to get past his emotionality and to be able to read, write, and comprehend schoolwork at grade level.

History:
Explosiveness, anger, and disorganization.
Crawl (9 months) Creep (unknown) Walk (11 months)

ND Evaluation:
Primarily left-handed – blueprint not established
Ear dominance mixed, slightly more to the right
Eye dominance primarily right
Foot dominance mixed
Processing significantly low
Visual inefficiencies
Stammers and physical tics
Primitive reflexes active
Lower-level organization poor
Neurological organization incomplete

The Strategy:
Reinforce and complete lower-level organization
Integrate primitive reflexes
Determine the blueprint
Subsequently, the blueprint presented right-side dominant
Align to right-side dominance
Increase processing
Eliminate visual inefficiencies and tics
Improve oral motor and speech
Organize the central nervous system

The Transformation: 24 months of ND (ended before graduation)
Right-side dominance near complete
Processing increased one developmental year
Visual inefficiencies – gone!
Stammer and tics – gone!
Academics doing well – above grade level
Neurological Organization – near complete

## *Irene: 14 years old*

Irene was 14 years old when we first met. She was struggling terribly in school, and despite her family going through an extremely stressful time in their life, her mother came in hoping to be able to help her daughter. For reasons beyond her mom's control, it would be three and a half years before I saw Irene again. A family friend, who had completed NDApproach programs with two of her children, as well as herself, offered to help Irene, who was now eighteen, with her plan. What a blessing, as the changes were incredible and life-changing!

Initial Evaluation Notes:
School is quite challenging, especially math. Reading comprehension tests at sixth-grade level, and math is at the third-grade level. Irene has a tough time communicating what she wants to say and often speaks without thinking. She doesn't like change or people crowding her, and she'd rather complain than reason through a matter.

History:
Induced, cord wrapped around her neck, meconium swallowed, blue
Appendectomy – 13 years
Crawl (unknown) Creep (unknown) Walk (unknown)

ND Evaluation:
Right-handed – blueprint presents left-side dominant
Ear and Eye dominance mixed, more to the left
Foot dominance mixed
Processing deficient and slow
Attention and focus – poor
Retention of information – poor
Visual inefficiencies
Primitive reflexes active
Lower-level organization incomplete

The Strategy:
Strengthen and complete lower-level organization
Integrate primitive reflexes
Align dominance to the left
Increase processing
Eliminate visual inefficiencies
Organize the central nervous system

The Transformation: 16 months of ND (graduated)
Left-side dominance 100% complete
Lower-level organization – complete
Primitive reflexes near complete
Processing superior
Organizational skills – excellent
Academically doing well – preparing for the GED
Communicating, expressing herself well – even in social settings
Focus and Attention – excellent
Confident, mature, calm
Visual inefficiencies – gone!
Neurological Organization – complete!

## Jacob: 12 years old

Jacob's mom had concerns about him since he was a toddler. He screamed frequently, had long-lasting outbursts, and intentionally banged his head. His mom was sure he would outgrow the negative behaviors, but only the head-banging stopped. The day came when she realized he was getting angrier, having meltdowns more often, and something pro-actively needed to be done to help him. He was brilliant, she told me, but his emotionality and poor behaviors were crippling his life.

Initial Evaluation Notes:
There are no academic concerns with Jacob; he is in the gifted and talented program at school, has straight A's, and recently scored 100 percent on both sections of the state standardized testing. All concerns revolve around his emotionality and behavior. He is determined, a hard worker, and very organized. Unfortunately, he is perfectionistic and extremely tough on himself when he makes a mistake or doesn't understand something. He likes routine and structure in his life, almost to an obsession. Tending to be anti-social, he keeps to himself, "zones out" often, and engages poorly with his family. He is angry, impulsive, rigid, and frequently displays his emotions in explosive outbursts.

History:
Asthma, allergies
Crawl (4 months) Creep (6 months) Walk (12 months)

ND Evaluation:
Right-handed – blueprint presented left-side dominant
Ear dominance mixed, slightly more to the right
Eye dominance firmly left
Foot dominance mixed
Processing fairly good
Visual inefficiencies
Primitive reflexes active
Lower-level organization incomplete
Neurological organization incomplete

The Strategy:
Reinforce and complete lower-level organization
Integrate primitive reflexes
Eliminate visual inefficiencies
Align to left-side dominance
Organize the central nervous system

The Transformation: 16 months of ND (graduated)
100% left-side dominant
Visual inefficiencies – gone!

Tested out of 8th grade into the dual high school and college program
Communication improved
Emotion and social concerns – gone!
Neurological Organization – complete

# Mini-SNAPSHOTS

### *15-year-old male, 22 months of ND (ended before graduation)*
Life before Neurological Organization:
Diagnosis: PDD-NOS
Tension tremors
Procrastination, incomplete work (chores and school)
Avoidance behaviors, disobedient
Doesn't offer information – needs to be "dragged out"
Joking, silly behavior at very inappropriate times

Life after an NDApproach Journey: (dominant hand-change near complete)
Smiling a lot
Much calmer
Confidence increased
Showing empathy for the first time
Voice modulation, tone natural sounding
PDD-NOS – gone!

### *22-year-old female, 19 months of ND (graduated)*
Life before Neurological Organization:
Poor at testing
Cannot multitask

Life after an NDApproach Journey: (dominant hand-change successful)
Alertness greatly improved
Maturity significantly increased
Much more assertive
Intuitively aware for the first time
Thinking things through substantially better

### *12-year-old male, 25 months of ND (graduated)*
Life before Neurological Organization:
Fine motor deficits
Extreme left/right confusion
Can be loud, clumsy, frustrates easily, likes to argue
Impulsive, disorganized, cannot follow directions
Seems lazy, no motivation
Doesn't pick up on social cues
Poor memory

Life after an NDApproach Journey: (dominant hand-change successful)
No longer experiencing left/right confusion
Listens, follows directions; focus significantly improved
Conversational skills greatly improved, finds words easily
Stuttering, mumbling, being loud – gone!
Impulsive, clumsy, frustration, argumentative – gone!
Memory great
Had resisted any kind of physical activity – now running 5k events'

## *9-year-old female, 24 months of ND (graduated)*

Life before Neurological Organization:
"Attitude" with mother
Unreasonable when emotional or argumentative
Talkative and bossy
Always convinced she is right
Frustration, rigidity, impulsive, explosive – severe
Tics – right shoulder and arm

Life after an NDApproach Journey: (dominant hand-change successful)
Maturing significantly
Interested in having friends
No longer argumentative, bossy
Frustration and rigidity – mild
"Attitude" with mother – gone!
Tics – gone!

## *10-year-old male, 21 months of ND (graduated)*

Life before Neurological Organization:
Academics difficult, retention poor
No interest in reading; must re-read material often to comprehend
Talks too loudly, except in school where he is extremely quiet
Frustrated, yet easy-going, sweet and laid back
Doesn't like challenges or being out of his comfort zone

Life after an NDApproach Journey: (dominant hand-change successful)
Maturity and confidence significantly increased
Misunderstanding words decreased
Following directions, attention, and listening skills substantially better
Good concentration and focus
Retains information well
Expresses thoughts well, volume of his voice appropriate
Articulation improved, no longer stammers or mutters
Adapts well in different groups and ages
Handles challenges well

### *13-year-old female, 17 months of ND (graduated)*
Life before Neurological Organization:
Struggles when given too many instructions
Disorganized and emotional
Auditory processing concerns

Life after an NDApproach Journey: (dominant hand-change successful)
Emotionally stable
Pleasant and enjoyable
Self-disciplined and organized

### *12-year-old male, 53 months of ND (graduated)*
Life before Neurological Organization:
Frustration continual, short attention span, rigid
Self-deprecating
Blames others for everything gone wrong
Makes up details regarding experiences, believes they are true
Auditory processing concerns
Multiple allergies – weekly shots in addition to daily medications

Life after an NDApproach Journey: (dominant hand-change successful)
Frustration and rigidity – gone!
Great attention span and increased maturity
Takes responsibility, socially appropriate
Self-deprecation – gone!
Awkward movements – gone!
Processing superior
No longer on medication or taking allergy shots

### *13-year-old female, 11 months of ND (graduated)*
Life before Neurological Organization:
Rigid and introverted
Bad attitude – constant
Negative – all the time

Life after an NDApproach Journey: (dominant hand-change unnecessary)
Organized and hard-working
Does well with taking notes, tests, remembers what is heard or read
Good attention span and focus
Reading is excellent
Dislikes change is the only negative noted

### *11-year-old male, 20 months of ND (graduated)*
Life before Neurological Organization:
Impulsive, explosive, disorganized

Lacks follow-through
No interest in having friends
Avoidance and procrastination
Tics
Dislikes reading

Life after an NDApproach Journey: (dominant hand-change successful)
Very even-keel, emotionally stable, calmer
Laid back and easy going
Staying controlled, even when upset
Gets over upsets more quickly
Less stress, anxiousness
More assertive socially
Greater self-expression, comfort with interactions
Asking for friends to come over
Tics decreased
Memory improved
Loves to read

### *7-year-old female, 31 months of ND (graduated)*

Life before Neurological Organization:
Behavior – wonderful
Concerns – coordination and posture
Wants to make sure she is neurologically organized

Life after an NDApproach Journey: (dominant hand-change successful)
Posture significantly improved
Coordination doing well
Neurological organization complete!

### *9-year-old male, 27 months of ND (ended before graduation)*

Life before Neurological Organization:
Anxiety and stress levels high, poor at testing
Continual self-talk, such as, "I'm a failure" and "I can't do it"
Poor self-control, poor situational awareness
Resists authority
Over-reactive, emotional yo-yo

Life after an NDApproach Journey: (dominant hand-change successful)
Behavior improved, significantly fewer tantrums
Maturity increased
Calmer
Decreased anxiety and depression
Emotional responses much improved

Four months after graduation: (dominant hand-change reverted)
Emotionality increased as INP decreased
Frustration higher
More aggressive
Gloomier, showing more interest in weapons and violent ideas

The family moved a few months later and never came back for further assessments. It doesn't mean they didn't finish on their own, which I hope is the case, but I never received a response when I attempted contact, so I simply do not know.

## *10-year-old female, 16 months of ND (ended before graduation)*

Life before Neurological Organization:
Diagnosis: ADD, Processing disorder
Obsessive behaviors – fiddles with hair, blows in hands, pinches skin
Constantly in motion, always needs to be touching something
Unaware of space
Focus poor, never finishes a project
Ignores people, no empathy
Overreacts, loses control
Anxious, frustrated, disorganized

Life after an NDApproach Journey: (dominant hand-change successful)
Calmer, controlling emotions better, much more pleasant overall
Frustration and moodiness significantly decreased
Maturity increased
Organization improved
Only one obsessive behavior left – slight hair twirling; the rest – gone!

Four months later: (significant regression in hand dominance)
All negative behaviors have increased
Emotionality increased
Feelings hurt often
Less cooperative

16 months later: final evaluation (ended before graduation)
Obsessive/compulsive behaviors significantly increased
Tics with shoulders and tongue have emerged
Rigidity – severe
"A year ago things were going well" – gone since reverting dominance

## *8-year-old male, 29 months of ND (graduated)*

Life before Neurological Organization:
Diagnosis: dyslexia, processing speed disorder
Reading, word-attack difficult

Significant reversals (written and visual)
Difficult to get him outside to play
Doesn't want to compete

Life after an NDApproach Journey: (dominant hand-change successful)
Reading is going well
Fluency significantly increased, word attack has improved
Reversals – gone!

## *48-year-old female, 20 months of ND (graduated)*
Life before Neurological Organization:
Reading is slow and makes tired
Memory declining
Motion sickness – severe
Sound sensitivity (crowds, noisy environments, background noise)
Desires to be organized, have better focus and learn with ease
Wants to have more energy.

Life after an NDApproach Journey: (dominant hand-change successful)
Short-term/Long-term memory significantly improved
Life-long motion sickness – gone!
Visual acuity improved – can now thread needles
Sound sensitivity – gone!

## *13-year-old male, 16 months of ND (graduated)*
Life before Neurological Organization:
Blanks out on tests
Takes too long to complete homework and tests
Stresses easily
Tends to be negative and disorganized
Lacks self-control and often blurts out in anger

Life after an NDApproach Journey: (dominant hand-change unnecessary)
Maturity significantly increased
Better control over emotions
Organization of thoughts improved
Disorganization significantly decreased
Significantly better with timed tests, homework completed quickly

## *6-year-old female, 15 months of ND (ended before graduation)*
Life before Neurological Organization:
Diagnosis: ADHD
Following directions, listening to others – difficult
Focus, sitting still – impossible
Hyperactive, impulsive, inattentive, emotional, frustration – severe

Life after an NDApproach Journey: (dominant hand-change successful)
Maturity significantly increased
Expressing thoughts, conversational skills significantly increased
Memory, attention, and listening to others substantially improved
Much calmer, distractibility decreased – able to sit still!
Extended family noting much-improved behavior
ADHD – gone!

## *13-year-old male, 24 months of ND (graduated)*

Life before Neurological Organization:
Diagnosis: Vision perceptual-motor disorder; color-blind
Lacks focus, hyperactive
Easily frustrated
Does not stay on task
Retention of information poor

Life after an NDApproach Journey: (dominant hand-change successful)
Maturity and follow-through significantly improved
Hyperactivity substantially decreased, slight fidgeting at times
Frustration – gone!
Attitude and focus considerably better
Calmer and much more positive
Talkative and interactive

## *9-year-old female, 106 months of ND (graduated)*

Life before Neurological Organization:
Diagnosis: Bartlet-Biedl syndrome (retinitis pigmentosa, night blindness, vision degeneration, and obesity)
Upsets easily, overly emotional, dislikes change
Destructive, aggressive, deliberately hurts others
Immature, disrespectful, talks back, lies, complains, disobeys

Life after an NDApproach Journey: (dominant hand change successful)
Significant weight loss – maintaining well
Over-emotionality – gone!
Destructiveness, lying, disliking change – gone!
Delightful to be with, great attitude, respectful
Interactions and communication appropriate; maturing well
Enjoys being with people
Kind, caring, compassionate, and thinks of others
Creates loom bands and does 1000-2000 piece puzzles by touch

## *24-month-old male, 24 months of ND (ongoing)*

Life before Neurological Organization:
Diagnosis: Down syndrome
The family wants to help their son reach his fullest potential

Life on an NDApproach Journey: (currently 16 years old)
Ninth-grade (math only accommodation) A/AB Honor Roll
Word recognition tests eleventh grade, the ninth month
Reading comprehension tests seventh grade, the ninth month
Processing skills – excellent
Conversational abilities – exceptional
Family and peer interactions – excellent

### *Four-month-old female, 87 months of ND (ongoing)*

Life before Neurological Organization:
Diagnosis: Down syndrome
The family wants to help their daughter reach her fullest potential

Life on an NDApproach Journey: (currently seven years old)
Reads fluently with excellent tonality, expression, and comprehension
Word recognition tests seventh grade
Math tests third grade, the second month
Reads music and plays the piano well
Focus and attention span – excellent!
Articulating well, especially when slow and careful
Conversational skills – excellent!
Very intuitive with language!
Social and behavioral ability – exceptional!
Loves playing checkers, board, and card games
Great balance, coordination, strength, and endurance
Loves hiking, swimming, and bike riding

I can go on and on bragging about our families and their journeys towards helping their children (or themselves) be the best that God created them to be. The families have been faithful and diligent, persevering through the ups and downs, all the while refusing to give up. Every story is unique and precious. I pray you were able to find hope and encouragement through this attempt at having you "look with my eyes."

There is not an exact way of working through an ND program, as you can see from the testimonies earlier in the book, and these shared "snapshots." Some families stay until completion, and others need to move on before everything gets resolved. Some, such as the last three journeys shared, are marathoners – they are in it for the duration. Wherever your child is, whatever they (and thus your family) is facing, there is hope.

Neurologically organizing the central nervous system eradicates learning labels and learning challenges. There is no way to overstate the essential need for aligning to the correct blueprint of each individual's neurological design. Yet, this is not being discussed or pursued in any other methodology, educational, or medical setting. The overwhelming number of "hand-changes" that I have witnessed causes great concern to me, as I know they represent just a small percentage of persons who are suffering needlessly because the "wrong" dominant hand has established. How can they even realize the possibility of the life-changing transformation possible for them if this information isn't more common-place and more broadly understood.

My prayer is for this book to open wide the door to unlocking the trapped and hidden potential of hundreds, thousands, and, yes, millions of lives. No matter what challenges you are facing, be encouraged; it is never too late, and rest assured, there is hope for the future!

# Epilogue

The work will go on because the needs will continue as long as this information isn't common knowledge – the imperative need for each person's brain to develop and organize according to their genetic pattern. By following each individual's blueprint, we can assure that our precious children and grandchildren can reach their fullest potential and live joyful, meaningful, and powerful lives.

I met with the Straus family days after completing the last chapter of this book. Charlotte Straus couldn't wait to have three of her children evaluated since hearing me speak at the ICHE (Illinois Christian Home Educators) annual conference. Alan, their 11-year-old son, adopted from Ethiopia, was very witty and fun to be around. However, he was also very negative and angry, especially when the subject related to school or a task he could not accomplish. Ned, their 14-year-old son adopted from Guatemala, is organized, excellent at any job with a built-in routine, but quick to blame others for things that are obviously his own fault. Both boys test extremely poor. Their third born, Helen, shared that when life is good – all is good. However, when life is hard, which frequently happens, she becomes super emotional and withdraws. Sometimes it takes days to recover. At 28, Helen is getting married in a few months and hopes that becoming neurologically organized will be valuable in her exciting new life. As in turns out, all three young people are going against the blueprint of their neurological design. Helen and Nathan are now switching from right to left dominance, with Ned going from left to right dominance. Charlotte just shook her head and said, "*I knew it! I knew it from the moment I heard you speak at the conference about issues that surface when people have not aligned to their correct side.*"

Then, just last week, the Blevins family flew in with two of their children for evaluations. Josiah, age 14, was a hoot to work with, and he made "sound effects" with everything he did. Mom Marcy said, "*Whatever is floating around in his head comes out of his mouth!*" He was non-stop motion and commotion. I loved every minute with him, even though it was head-spinning. Josiah, diagnosed with dyslexia at six, has displayed significant emotional and behavioral issues for years, which had always been blamed on dyslexia. His sister, Bethany, suffered from severe depression, anxiety, and post-traumatic stress disorder. The trauma started for her in-utero with a traumatic birth, then continued at 12-years-old with a dirt bike accident, and then was catapulted further when she was 17, by a major car accident. She told me she used to pull her eyelashes out to cope with her stress and anxiety. However, because she didn't like how that looked, she switched to pulling her eyebrows out – which she currently is still doing. Both Josiah and Bethany had not aligned to their appropriate dominant side.

As with Charlotte, Marcy knew her children were going the wrong way with their dominance from the moment she heard me discuss this topic at a conference. Then she added, "*I have one more at home who is using the wrong side, too – my18-year-old son, Kevin. If I can convince him, you'll be seeing him, too.*" I evaluated Kevin a couple of days ago. Marcy was correct he was going against his blueprint, and Kevin now has hope.

Last month we received the following email from a family we formerly worked with. I include this email as a reminder that it is NEVER too late to organize the central nervous system and have life-long positive changes that impact the quality and trajectory of your life or your child's life.

> *Hi Linda,*
>
> *You helped my son, Brody, back in 2011 when he was 10 years old. In addition to the program you designed, you highly suggested that he convert from right handed to left handed. Well, he's 20 years old right now and his dysgraphia and ADHD seem to be frustrating him more often. He's now ready to really commit to switching to the left hand.*
>
> *We would like to know if you are able to help him and, if so, what we need to do to make this happen.*
>
> *Thank you.*

**Yes! Yes! Yes! We can help!**

The stories will continue. There will be heartwarming, happy-ending stories of children and adults organizing their neurological systems and radically changing their lives for the better. We will have the privilege and honor of walking next to many families as they help their children be the best person

God created them to be. We will continue to share the stories of these precious families and their journeys from hopelessness, desperation, and uncertainty to courage, perseverance, and victory. For anyone struggling in the midst of it "all," please hear this life-sustaining truth once more…

> *For I know the plans I have for you, declares the Lord.*
> *Plans to help you and not to harm you.*
> *Plans to give you a hope and a future.*
>
> Jeremiah 29:11 – New International Version

My husband and I found neurodevelopmental intervention because of our son, Scott, who was born with Down syndrome. The NDApproach radically changed Scott's life, and thus our lives, for the better. At nearly 14, Scott was locked in his "own world" until we found out you could stimulate the brain and produce incredible changes in function, ability, and quality of life. We learned that it's all about the brain, and that knowledge and experience created a passion in us to share this information with others. You can find out more specifics on this approach, how to search for root causes of negative issues and challenges disrupting your loved one's life (or yours), and then learn what and how to apply appropriate stimulation to correct these inefficiencies in my first book, *"The NeuroDevelopmental Approach"* … *"There is Hope And A Future."*

**May God bless your journey and the stories you are creating.**

# About the Author

Lee and Linda Kane entered the field of special needs in 1977 with the birth of their oldest son, Scott. Scott was born with Down syndrome and their pediatrician recommended institutionalizing him by the age of two. Refusing to even consider this, Lee and Linda ventured out on their own seeking help for their son. They found the NeuroDevelopmental Approach in 1989 and had dramatic results. Scott transformed from being totally in his own world to becoming an active, engaging, semi-independent young man.

Realizing the life-changing effects of this approach, Linda entered into an eight-year apprenticeship in the neurodevelopmental field. Additionally, she has extensive training in Behavioral Management, Sound Therapy, Primitive/Postural Reflexes and Feeding/Oral Motor Therapy.

It became Lee's and Linda's passion to share the NeuroDevelopmental Approach with other families. This passion led to their founding "*Hope And A Future*" in September, 1999. *Hope And A Future* guides families by giving them the expertise for working with the specific, individual needs of their child – no matter what type of challenges they are facing.